OUT OF THE WILDERNESS

with Alan Lee

WILLOW BOOKS
Collins
8 Grafton Street, London W1
1985

Willow Books
William Collins Sons & Co. Ltd
London · Glasgow · Sydney · Auckland
Toronto · Johannesburg

First published 1985

BRITISH LIBRARY CATALOGUING IN PUBLICATION DATA
Gooch, Graham
Out of the wilderness.
1. Cricket – South Africa 2. Cricket – England
I. Title II. Lee, Alan, *1954–*
796.35′865 GV928.S/

ISBN 0 00 218178 9

Set in Linotron Plantin by
Rowland Phototypesetting Ltd
Bury St Edmunds, Suffolk
Printed in Great Britain by
St Edmundsbury Press, Bury St Edmunds, Suffolk

Contents

1
Something different

Boredom gets the blame for many of modern society's problems. We are told it causes teenagers to become soccer louts, the unemployed to become depressants and the elderly to feel suicidal. All of which makes my claims to sympathy look pretty thin.

I was bored, even disillusioned, on an England cricket tour of India. The feeling helped influence me to make a decision which brought temporary turmoil to my life. I went to South Africa on a secret, private tour. Cricket officialdom did not approve. My punishment was three years in the wilderness away from international cricket.

'No regrets' might now be my motto, because in truth I do not think the sentence has harmed me, however much I may sometimes have missed the flowing adrenalin, the atmosphere and the unsurpassed sense of pride which only a Test match can provide for a cricketer. I cannot honestly open this account with a statement of remorse, because I feel none. In my own mind I am convinced I did nothing wrong, that my actions were right for my mood and my circumstances at the time and that, if political considerations had not been paramount, the cricket authorities of this country would probably have been more supportive than savage in their pronouncements on the matter.

With that said, however, I must also concede that I might never have gone to the outlawed country if the 1981–82 trip to India had been stimulating, successful or preferably both. Instead, it came as a dire disillusionment to one who had felt he would never tire of international cricket. During that winter of unspeakably tedious cricket and endless dull evenings, I slipped into the type of depression I would not have considered possible while playing for England. So I went to South Africa.

It is perfectly possible I would have taken the same decision if

England had won gloriously in England. I just don't know for sure. Certainly, I was in favour of tours being made to South Africa, of the barriers being broken down and apartheid being challenged by direct contact rather than ostracism. I felt that the boycott of South Africa by sporting teams had been partially successful over a period of ten or 12 years but that the time had come to test out their claims of multi-racial conditions in the only positive way available – by going out there to play against them.

I was not naïve enough to imagine the cricket authorities would be beside themselves with joy. I was, however, naïve enough to think that the tour would be treated on its merits as a sporting venture, not a political issue. I was wrong.

The South African saga was a lengthy one, stretching back more than a year, to the first week of February 1981. England were in Port of Spain, Trinidad, for the First Test of what turned out to be a fraught series against West Indies. Oddly enough, we were experiencing a different type of political row, emanating from the omission of Trinidadian Deryck Murray from the West Indies side. The locals would not accept that this was a logical decision based on Murray's advancing years and declining form. Trinidad cricket officials boycotted the eve-of-Test board dinner, demonstrations were staged outside the ground and, on the first morning of the match, it was discovered that the pitch had been sabotaged. And this, apparently, was provoked by nothing more than inter-island jealousies! To make matters appreciably worse for an England party already handicapped by poor weather disrupting our practice and by an injury to our best bowler, Bob Willis, we were thrashed by an innings when the game did finally get underway.

It was clearly not the best time to talk business, and perhaps that was why none of us discovered at that stage the identity of the tall, dark man who spent some time with Geoff Boycott at the Hilton Hotel where we were staying. The tour had taken a scarcely believable turn for the worse by the time I found out that Boycott's friend had been a man named Peter Cooke, a South African businessman and entrepreneur travelling on a British passport.

We had moved on to Guyana, ostensibly the venue for the Second Test. How ironic it is that we left that country rapidly, thankfully and without setting foot on the Bourda ground, following the deportation order which was served on Willis's replacement, Robin Jackman. Robin's crime was to have spent several winters coaching in South Africa yet, during the very days that the crisis surrounding him was at its peak, secret talks were taking place with the long-term aim of taking a team to South Africa.

Boycott asked five other members of the touring team to a meeting in his room at Pegasus Hotel, which had become little more than a prison to us while the politicians decreed our future. Ian Botham, our captain, was present, along with David Gower, John Emburey, Graham Dilley and myself. No doubt Willis would also have been invited, but he had already gone home for surgery on his troublesome knee.

We were told of Boycott's discussions with Peter Cooke who, it transpired, was an old friend of Geoff's from his regular working holidays in Johannesburg. Cooke had flown to Trinidad specifically to sound out Boycott about the possibility of raising a side to tour South Africa. Boycott was now, in turn, putting the proposal before us.

In truth, the idea was not even flat on the drawing-board at that stage. We heard that there was a potential backer for such an event, which turned out to be the Holiday Inn hotel chain, and that the possible dates were either October 1981 or March 1982 – in other words, to avoid clashing with any England commitments.

None of us, Boycott apart, had ever met Peter Cooke and, looking back, I suppose we regarded the prospect with a certain scepticism. It was, after all, nothing particularly new. Trips to South Africa were often being mooted. Vast sums of money were frequently spoken of. But, up to then, only the officially blessed and strictly private parties taken out by the likes of Derrick Robins had ever managed to pass the talking stage. So when Boycott asked each of us to sign a hand-written letter confirming our interest in the scheme, no more and no less, there seemed no reason for alarm or apprehension – indeed, no real reason to suppose it would ever go much farther. It seemed to be Boycott's appointed task to sound out the best of the English talent and inform Peter Cooke of his results. Already, we understood, Alan Knott had been approached and expressed interest, and there were likely to be more feelers put out in the weeks to follow.

The basics of the projected visit were very vague. We were given no hint as to what shape the cricket might take – for all we knew it could have ended up as a double-wicket tournament or a couple of World XIs playing against each other. There was never any mention at this juncture of the fact that we would be playing for an England XI. If there had been, I would immediately have dropped my interest as I did not at any time see the venture as a threat to Test matches, or even a substitute version.

Money matters were scarcely raised at this initial meeting, although Boycott's outline of the scheme made it pretty clear we were not talking about peanuts. Frankly, I do not think international cricketers would consider a tour of South Africa for anything but substantial reward while present circumstances prevail, because there is very clearly an element of risk. None of us, either at that stage or much later, could have known quite what a severe line would be taken against us for going, but we would have needed to be blinkered to believe such a trip would pass unnoticed.

My line throughout all the meetings we attended over the next 12 months was that I was not against going to South Africa if the majority of the England side went. If only two or three players had signed up to play there in a major tournament, they would certainly have been singled out for punishment; if the whole team went, action against them would have been very much more difficult and painful to implement.

Geoff told us that the matter must remain confidential, even from other members of the tour party. And that was how it was to stay. Nothing happened during the remainder of that trip to make me think the venture was anything more than another promoter's pipe-dream. To be honest, we were all too preoccupied with the problems which seemed to pile up for us in the Caribbean to give too much thought to anything else. We came back a beaten team, but draws in the last two Tests had done much to restore our pride and, on a personal note, my century in the final game at Kingston represented my best innings for England. The press was flattering – Boycott and Gooch should be England's openers for years to come, the papers chorused . . . but it was not to be.

By the middle of the following summer's Ashes series against Australia, I had completely lost form at Test level and it came as no surprise at all when I was dropped from the England side for the final match of the rubber which had captivated the nation. It had been memorable to be part of those stirring wins at Headingley, Edgbaston and Old Trafford and to witness at close quarters the almost miraculous performances of Ian Botham and Bob Willis. It was not easy to slip back into county cricket directly afterwards, but I knew my form did not merit selection and consoled myself with the thought that a few big scores for Essex in the closing weeks of the season would guarantee my place on the coming trip to India and Sri Lanka. Which is exactly what happened.

I had already been named in the party – and, to my great delight, Keith Fletcher had been brought back as captain – when Boycott phoned to tell me that things had begun to move. It came as something of a surprise because the only occasion when South Africa hit the news that summer was the disclosure that John Edrich, an England selector, had been recruiting players for a possible trip there. He had not approached me, and it appeared that his efforts had nothing to do with the proposed tour in which I was already tentatively involved, but this news sparked off some frenzied activity in the newspapers for a week or so, rumour following speculation following gossip. South Africa was an emotive subject. It still is.

Boycott's message was that the organizers of our trip were coming to England and wanted to meet with interested players. We fixed the date for a Sunday in October, the meeting place to be the Holiday Inn Hotel in Kensington. It felt wintry cold that day. I wore my sheepskin wrapped tightly around me as Brenda and I walked from our car to the hotel. I wanted Brenda to be at the meeting with me, because her opinion of the trip was important. In the lobby I met Mike Gatting and Graham Dilley, both with their wives, and I was slightly surprised to discover that they were the only two other players present. It later transpired that discussions were taking place at different locations around the country during that week as the nucleus of a squad was put together, on paper at least.

Mike and Graham left their wives in the lobby when we went upstairs to meet Peter Cooke for the first time. With him was Stuart Banner, a Scotsman introduced to us as the marketing director of Holiday Inns for Southern Africa. Cooke was a sturdy man in his late thirties, confident and self-assured. My first impressions were not good, in fact I thought him a rather shady character, but those doubts disappeared when I came to know him better, much later in the story.

It was the Holiday Inns man who did most of the talking, as the appointed propaganda spokesman for the potential sponsors. He explained the fundamental details of the proposal, such as they were. It remained unclear just who we would be playing for if we agreed to go, but it would come under the Holiday Inns banner. At this stage, it seemed to me most likely that it would turn out to be something unspecific, like a World XI, but Banner told us very firmly that they aimed to attract all the major English names and would be speaking to Botham and Gower in the coming days.

He was at pains to point out that Holiday Inns would be investing about £500,000 in the tour, which made us all sit up rather wide-eyed and helped to drum home the message that this was no fly-by-night affair but a genuine attempt to put on authentic high-quality cricket. It was not at the time mentioned that we would be playing against a representative South African side, but then perhaps we should have worked that out.

When Peter Cooke spoke, he endorsed Banner's comments by crediting Holiday Inns with the reputation of being the best and most prestigious sponsors in South Africa. He told us that the tour was pencilled in for the following March, immediately at the end of England's winter commitments, and he stressed the importance of secrecy. In fact he did rather more. So essential was it that the plans remained under wraps that he had gone to the extent of using an off-the-shelf company called Oxychem, through which the tour was to be administered. All players would be contracted to Oxychem rather than to any cricketing body, in order to divert attention.

Fees were discussed in vague terms but Peter Cooke undertook to send each of us a sample contract for perusal. No pressure was put upon us, indeed the meeting was little more than a talking shop, but in hindsight I went home feeling rather apprehensive. The demands for subterfuge, sealed lips and almost deception worried me. I could not be sure how genuine these men were and I realized that I was teetering on the brink of the unknown.

I might quite easily have made up my mind there and then to refuse all the offers and, no doubt, purge myself in the eyes of cricket officialdom if and when their current state of blissful ignorance was interrupted. It would, after all, have been much the easiest thing to do. Just say no, I told myself, and be rid of the inevitable worries associated with such a secretive venture. Brenda had already made up her mind. She did not want me to go. Being a naturally cautious, conservative person, she foresaw perils and pressures of a magnitude I did not wish to contemplate. She feared for me, and she was undoubtedly suspicious of the motives behind the idea, perhaps reading into them elements of propaganda and exploitation which, only time would prove, were not there. We knew by then that any such tour would be bound to cause great publicity, some of it of a vitriolic and even vindictive nature. I had to weigh up the reasons for going, both moral and financial, against the predicament in which it might place my family and myself.

I have to say that I was not seriously influenced by the Test and County Cricket Board's recent pronouncements on the issue. Probably provoked by the rumours concerning John Edrich's activities and the possibility which had existed for some years that a private promoter might put together a team to tour South Africa, the board had composed and circulated what must be termed a warning letter to every contracted county cricketer. While being necessarily vague and sketchy when it came to threats of punishment, there was really no mistaking the intention to deter. It was delivered to the Essex players during a home match by our secretary Peter Edwards and, in the normal fashion with such missives, it was read and discussed in the dressing-room. My clearest memory is that some of the players regarded it as a cheek and that at least onc was incensed enough to throw the letter into the waste-paper bin immediately he had read it. Every employer is entitled to try to protect his interests, but to be dictating – and in threatening terms – to players over what they were permitted to do during the off-season was undoubtedly an imposition, because county players are in paid employment only from 1 April to 25 September each year. Outside that period, the TCCB claims no responsibility for players not fortunate enough to be selected for official tours and, while some are retained in outside jobs and others go abroad to coach, there is still a proportion of cricketers forced to resort to the dole each winter. If the board had, over the years, been willing or able to concern itself with the welfare of players during off-season periods, its warning might have seemed less one-sided.

It certainly failed to make me feel I should not go to South Africa. What it did instead was persuade me to seek an alteration in my county contract, which used to state that, for instance, I was contracted 'for a period of three years'. Under those terms, Essex could theoretically have been awkward when I went to South Africa without consulting them, despite the fact that they were not paying me during that time. I have since stipulated that my contract should run only from April to September each year – the months for which I receive a salary.

Such considerations, however, still seemed remote, if not irrelevant, as the winter evenings drew in and the tour party for India assembled at Lord's, late in 1981. For the time being, I had delayed my decision. I remained to be convinced one way or the other. Probably, I remained to be convinced that the tour would progress to a point where a decision was necessary.

Already, there had been another irony in a story which was to be littered with them. For while Geoff Boycott was acting as go-between in the recruitment of English cricketers by Peter Cooke, he was being asked to renounce his previous links with South Africa in order that the trip to India could go ahead. There had been objections from India over the inclusion of Boycott and Geoff Cook in our tour party. I do not know whether these were inspired by an anti-apartheid group such as SANROC, whose frequently published blacklist often seems to be compiled on rather tenuous grounds, but Boycott had in recent years never done more than visit Johannesburg on holiday. Cook, having graduated to Test cricket late in his career, had spent three winters playing Currie Cup cricket for Eastern Province, where incidentally he had improved his best-ever score and made a favourable impression with everyone concerned. This, however, did not contravene the Test and County Cricket Board's guidelines on South Africa and they made it plain to India that they were not prepared to accommodate their objections by omitting either Boycott or Cook.

For some weeks, the entire tour hung in the balance, and the person I most felt for during that time was Keith Fletcher. For so long he had waited in the wilderness for a recall to Test cricket. Now he had achieved it in the ultimate role of captain, only to find that his pedestal might be whipped from under him virtually before he had got his balance. I know how much it meant to him that the tour should go ahead and it was 'Fletch' I thought of immediately when it was announced that the matter had been amicably resolved. I believe Boycott and Cook agreed to make statements of their opposition to apartheid. The Indian request that they should also promise never to return to South Africa was refused which, in Boycott's case at least, saved some later embarrassment.

The on-field events of that tour are very simply related. We lost the First Test in Bombay, never batting well enough to counter-act some dubious umpiring, and from then on any chance we might have had of getting back in the series was killed by the most negative tactics I have ever encountered.

The off-field events take much more explaining and, even now, some of what happened may come as a surprise to a number of the players on the trip – not least to the captain who, despite later official suspicion to the contrary, remained utterly unaware of the discussions going on around him and the plan to leave for South Africa virtually as soon as the tour ended. 'Fletch' was kept in the dark for his own good. If he had been party to the scheme, he may well have felt obliged to honour the unwritten moral terms of his position and report the matter to the tour manager, Raman Subba Row, from whence it would have been only a phone call away from Lord's and a monumental leak. We did not want Keith to be put in such an invidious situation, where he would have to make a choice between loyalty to friends and team-mates and loyalty to his job and employers. As things turned out, we probably did him a disservice as he was the biggest loser from the whole affair. But at the time, it was certainly the right thing to do, and the meetings of the involved and interested players were conducted in complete secrecy, something which was often extremely difficult to achieve.

Take the first gathering of the tour. We were staying at the palatial Taj Mahal Hotel in Bombay for the duration of the First Test. Players habitually complain about the standard of accommodation in India, some of which is primitive and unwelcoming in the extreme, but I doubt if anyone will ever moan about the Taj, where the rooms, food and service are a match for any hotel in the world. It also happens to be extremely large and rambling, which for the purposes of organizing an undercover meeting is just as well. Word reached me that Peter Cooke had arranged for an agent to fly to Bombay. His name was Peter Venison, a South African-born entrepreneur now living in New York, and he managed to arrive, stay for a week, and leave again without, to my knowledge, arousing any comment.

One evening during the Test match he asked a group of players to come to his room. This might seem simple enough until one understands the rituals of touring. Other than the captain, and sometimes the senior professional, players always share, two to a room, when on tour, and in many cases this created the problem of one player in a room having been invited to the meeting while the other had not. It is customary, at the end of a day's play, for each pair of 'roomies' to go back and wind down for an hour or so, during which they will undoubtedly discuss social plans for the evening ahead. I can only imagine some of the spurious excuses which were invented to justify one player slipping away alone, but somehow it passed off without comment.

The seven players who attended that meeting were David Gower, Ian Botham, Bob Willis, Graham Dilley, John Emburey, Boycott and myself – in other words, the group initially approached by Boycott during the Caribbean tour, plus Willis. Mike Gatting had apparently pulled out following that Sunday afternoon meeting with Peter Cooke in London, explaining that he was anxious about reaction to the tour and about the possible effect on a sports shop business he had only recently launched. A drop-out at such an early stage was a disappointment to me, given my view that the venture depended largely on a high proportion of the England team being in agreement, but Mike had decided quite reasonably that his personal circumstances would not benefit from going and, moreover, he respected the confidential nature of the process even when he ceased to be involved.

The Bombay meeting was the most detailed we had at any stage during the preliminaries to the trip. Peter Venison had arrived armed with a lot of detail in areas which had previously been cloudy, particularly the shape of the itinerary and the size of the fees. He put definite proposals before us regarding the number of matches we would be expected to play and it was now made clear that, whatever the title of the team, it was intended to be dominated by English players. Figures of up to £50,000 were now put forward for a month's cricket, although no guarantees were given that every player would be paid as much.

There was by now a plain awareness within the interested group that the flak would fly if the trip went ahead as planned. I do not know if anyone expected to be banned from Test cricket for going, but it was uppermost in everyone's mind that such an obviously controversial happening would have a number of repercussions and that consequently a certain amount of security was needed as additional enticement. A one-off trip was unattractive. Deals involving two or even three years were what the players wanted, and Peter Venison was asked to report back on this. A lot of questions were asked during the meeting and a lot of different views were put forward. Each player had his individual decision to make based on his personal feelings and his long-term future but, in the wake of these discussions, a clearer picture began to emerge of the likely runners and the probable scratchings.

The cast list was something like this. Boycott, being partly committed, was naturally keen to push the thing through; Emburey, not guaranteed an England place and not enjoying himself in India, was very interested; Willis, evidently close to the end of his Test career, seemed enthusiastic.

But there was nothing like the unanimity I had been hoping for.

Gower told me soon after the meeting that he could be discounted, and I was not entirely surprised to hear it. I had always felt he was basically unsympathetic to South Africa and he explained that he now had a lot of friends and contacts in the West Indies and did not wish to alienate them. That was one of the biggest names out, and there was another to follow.

Ian Botham was the biggest fish of all, so far as the organizers were concerned, and they later showed to just what lengths they were prepared to go to to catch him. But, to be fair to Ian, he also had more factors to consider than anyone else because of his numerous lucrative advertising and commercial deals, ostensibly outside the game but in all probability linked to his continued presence in the England team.

When we flew to Bangalore for the Second Test match, Ian was joined by his agent, Reg Hayter, and his solicitor, Alan Herd. I believe that Peter Cooke and his colleagues had been keen that they should come out from England to advise Ian – a gamble on the South Africans' behalf and one which backfired, because I assume their advice to their client was to refuse all offers. Ian told me later that he would have contravened or jeopardized a lot of contracts if he had gone and that, financially, it was not worth his while. I respected that decision, just as I respected the motives of anyone who stated he did go entirely for the money involved. Cricketers, in this regard, should not be seen as different, or more morally perfect, than any other businessmen; if a deal, legal and legitimate, is put before them by which they can substantially increase their income, I see no good reason why they should not take it up. Clichéd though it has now become, I will repeat the fact that no one questions, much less vilifies, the hundreds of British industries with interests in South Africa on a vast scale.

While I could not blame Ian for taking the negative decision on financial grounds, it surprised me to read, much later, that he had chosen not to go because of his friendship with Viv Richards. Indeed, in his personal column in *The Sun* on 3 March 1982 – four days after our party left for South Africa – Botham described his feelings about the offer like this: 'One thought kept flashing across my mind – I could never have looked my mate Viv Richards in the eye this season.' He did admit: 'I thought long and hard about the offer. At one point I tried to convince myself that I should make the trip to build bridges for black sportsmen in South Africa.' But Ian concluded: 'I didn't want to risk my Test career and, quite frankly, I am surprised that certain others have chosen to do just that. I had to consider my own future, the future of Kathy and the children . . . and the future of English cricket itself.' I have no doubt that this is all true but not once did Ian so much as hint that there was a financial consideration as well. I have always been a friend of Ian's and I hope I always will be, but on this issue I could not understand why he did not come out with the entire story.

That leaves Graham Dilley, the youngest of the seven tourists involved and, I think, the most impressionable. I have few doubts in my own mind that Graham would have been prepared to go on the trip if the other six had all agreed. But, understandably anxious about his future and still barely established in the Test side, I suppose he was influenced by the withdrawal of Gatting, Botham and Gower and decided to run with the pack.

Over the course of a few weeks these decisions were transmitted to Peter Cooke's office in South Africa and I could well imagine the consternation being expressed there. Cooke's ideal would have been to obtain the services of the best dozen English players. He could sustain the operation with one or two refusals, but commercial backers demand big names for their money and the loss of Gower and Botham put the whole show at risk. We did not know it at the time, but Holiday Inns, whose representative had been so bullish about the tour those few short weeks earlier, withdrew their offer of sponsorship when the news reached them.

So the big, brave concept now lay close to ruin. Not only had two of its star names left the cast, but the money had vanished too. If it had happened to a film crew on location the outcome would surely have been to abandon the whole thing, and for some weeks, while we battled against the boredom in India, it began to seem that this was what had happened. We had been told by our South Africa contacts to always refer to the tour plans by a codename. 'Chess match' was the phrase they came up with, and I expect there were one or two blank looks among our own players in India when they overheard a reference to it. But it was also to be used whenever we made contact, by telephone or telex, with any one of the tour's organizers. As we moved on via Delhi to Calcutta and Madras, however, communications dried up and the codewords became virtually redundant.

I suspected that the tour may have collapsed. And I have to admit that by that stage I would not have been distressed if it had. My own views about the venture had never reached a state of utter conviction, one way or the other, but I had been ready to join up if the support from other players was good and the terms of the contract were right. Now that the potential tour party was beginning to look appreciably short of full strength, however, I was wobbling even more. If I had been asked then for a definite decision, I would have said no.

2
Stratagems and spoils

Geoff Boycott made himself unpopular when he went home early from India. In fact I have never experienced such wholesale condemnation of one player by team-mates. But I cannot subscribe to the commonly-held suspicion that he returned to England purely to supervise plans for the South African trip. For one thing, I feel confident I would have known about it if that had been his plan – and there is no way I would have condoned such a retreat from an England tour. For another, there was by that stage little left for him to do. He had carried off the role of middle-man between organizers and players but it was not his brief to talk money or to negotiate over the itinerary, much less to search for a new sponsor.

No, my opinion of the reasons for his going are quite simplistic. In Delhi, during the Third Test, he had achieved one of his greatest ambitions in becoming the highest-scoring batsman in Test history. After that, I believe interest in the tour deserted him and instead of fighting it through, as the rest of us were obliged to do, he gave up and decided he would be better off at home. He did fall ill, of course, soon after his innings in Delhi in fact. But virtually everyone in the party was ill at some stage of the tour – it is simply an occupational hazard for an Englishman touring an eastern country – and no one else made the fuss that Geoffrey did. His sortie onto the golf course in Calcutta, while we were enduring 90-degree heat in the field, was just the straw that broke the camel's back. Whether he was officially sent home is immaterial; if he had stayed I believe he would not have been in the right frame of mind for the rest of the tour.

In one sense, however, I thought he was to be envied. I would love to have gone home by that stage of the tour. India, as I had feared from the outset of the trip, did not suit me. I did not get on with Indian food, much less the way they played their cricket.

'Fletch' would repeatedly tell us to think positively, to put the doubtful umpiring out of our minds and concentrate on trying to win – but then 'Fletch' knocked off a bail in Bangalore when he was given out, the ultimate proof of how hard it was for us all.

John Emburey and I agreed that it was the worst of the tours we had been on, and we were not the only players to feel that way. There was a good deal of moaning and a fair amount of depression. For all the effort put in by captain and manager, it was not a memorably happy tour in any respect . . . and perhaps that is why I remained interested in a trip to South Africa even when most of my instincts told me I should join the ranks of those to reject the offer.

It was in Delhi that we feared the secrecy system had sprung a leak. During a team meeting of otherwise routine nature, Raman Subba Row said that rumours had come to his attention concerning a projected visit to South Africa. He asked if anyone had heard of this. Nobody said a word. It could, of course, be said that our silence was in itself a lie, and I cannot pretend to be proud of deceiving a manager for whom I had nothing but respect. But what else could we do? It was to prevent the plans reaching his ears that the secrecy had been so strict – how could we now meekly own up to the plot and merely wait for the inevitable phone call informing Lords's of the matter. Loopholes would have been closed, a great fuss would have been caused and no one would have benefited. We had to keep quiet and hope that it would be considered a false alarm and rapidly forgotten. It was.

I was still uncommitted to the venture myself when we reached Kanpur for the final Test. Our base was a hotel called the Meghdoot, which is no slum but also no Taj Mahal, and, with Kanpur striking my eyes as a dreary and even more crowded version of Calcutta, a place I had not loved anyway, my mood was not exactly effervescent when a bellboy called me to the telephone.

I took the call on the phone which stood on the reception desk, just as a group of about a dozen Indians set about trying to check in with as much noise as they could muster. Down a very crackly line I could just about distinguish my caller as Martin Locke, another colleague of Peter Cooke. Martin, a former disc jockey turned sports commentator, was phoning to explain that, although Holiday Inns had pulled out and the tour currently had no backer, the South African Cricket Union had hinted that they might be able to find one if a team of appropriate quality could still be put together. He wanted to know the names of those still interested and, understandably, to press ahead with plans as the projected starting date was now only a month ahead. This would have been all very well if I had taken the call in my room. It would also not have been so bad on a clear line. But in the prevailing noise around the desk I had to raise my voice and yell my answers to Martin's questions while an interested crowd, which included more than one British pressman, stood by. Fortunately, I was able to use the 'Chess match' code and make my answers as ambiguous to outsiders as possible but, in hindsight, it was a comical scene.

The answer to Martin Locke's questions were not what he wanted to hear. Interest among the players had waned over the previous few weeks of silence and needed reviving if they were to get the tour off the ground. What is more, my wife Brenda had arrived for the last stages of the trip and was still set against my going. I made up my mind in Kanpur that she was right. I telexed South Africa and informed the organizers that I was very doubtful.

Perhaps the truth of it is I had cold feet. The enormity of what was about to happen had certainly filtered through by this stage. Months of secrecy had taken its toll and I wondered if there was any point in submitting to the certainty of a hostile reaction from the cricket authorities and the possibility of opposition from friends and family. I still considered that the tour would achieve more good than harm if it went ahead but, with the list of non-starters growing, I could see a situation developing in which English cricketers might be catagorized heroes and villains . . . and, given the choice, very few people want to be thought a villain.

With my mind virtually made up, and the Indian series drawing to its painfully tedious close – a 1–0 win to the Indians with five Tests drawn – Brenda and I decided we would like to have a holiday on the way home from our short stop in Sri Lanka. Both of us were keen to go back to Cape Town, where we had enjoyed ourselves greatly when I played for the Green Point club in the winter of

1975–76, and I went to ask Raman if it was possible to change my air ticket and allow for a stopover in Johannesburg, from where we could fly on to Cape Town. I was uncomfortably aware how suspicious this must have sounded and not at all surprised when Raman raised his eyebrows at the request. But I assured him the genuine intention was to have a holiday and meet up with old friends, and I was telling the absolute truth. Weeks later, when he heard of the South African tour getting underway, Raman must have believed I was trying to pull the wool over his eyes, and I actually wrote to him to apologise for the embarrassment and stressed that it was nothing but coincidence. I am sure, however, that he must have thought badly of me.

Quite what would have happened if we had been able to arrange that holiday I am not sure. But it turned out to be impossible to alter the tickets and so Brenda and I resigned ourselves to flying directly home and then, perhaps, snatching a break somewhere in Europe before the English season began.

In Colombo, however, I changed my mind again. Perhaps it was through spending so much time with John Emburey, who had made up his mind about the South African tour. Or perhaps it was a combination of insecurity – feeling that my Test place was anything but safe – and naïvety in believing we would not be banned anyway. Whatever the reasons, I decided to send another telex to Johannesburg intimating that I was still interested in the project – but only under certain conditions. I knew that the players on tour who had been approached to go had all, with the possible exception of Boycott, been offered the same fee. I was now asking them for considerably more. I also stipulated that I was only prepared to play if they could guarantee that our team would not be advertised as representing England.

Somewhat to my surprise, Peter Cooke rapidly telexed back his agreement to my conditions. I had mixed feelings. In a sense it had been a calculated gamble on my part to make such demands. I couldn't lose either way. If they agreed, I had secured a very favourable deal; if they disagreed, I simply wouldn't go. Call it a form of blackmail if you like, but at the time it never struck me that way. It was only much later, when at a safe distance I was able to piece together the full sequence of events, that I realized I could probably have asked for twice the figure I did, and still they would have agreed. The fact is, their tour was falling apart and they could not afford to lose any more players from their original priority list. They were prepared to go to great lengths in their desperation to maintain a squad of suitable strength to convince the South African Cricket Union that they had a package worth backing financially, because without that backing they were absolutely sunk.

So I was committed. Having made extra demands and been accommodated, I could hardly back out again now. And, with Boycott absent and Botham and Gower not involved, I found myself being used increasingly as the link between promoters and players. The frequency of phone calls increased rapidly during our stay in Colombo. John Emburey and I were both with our wives and had adjoining rooms, so if Peter Cooke or Martin Locke wanted to check a point or contact a player they would always come to one or other of us.

More players were obviously needed to make up a workable squad. From those originally approached, Boycott, Gooch, Emburey and Willis remained. We learned that Alan Knott, Peter Willey, Wayne Larkins, Mike Hendrick and Chris Old, none of whom were on our tour, had all been successfully approached. So now the intention was to sound out the rest of the England squad with the exception of Keith Fletcher, for reasons I have already outlined, and the two wicketkeepers, Bob Taylor and Jack Richards, because with Knott already signed up they were not needed.

So far as I am aware, John Emburey and I spoke to the rest of the players between us, and the results were as follows. Paul Allott and Chris Tavaré declined, Allott giving the reason that he was very new to Test cricket and did not want to put his place in jeopardy so soon. Geoff Cook would not commit himself. Derek Underwood, no doubt believing his England days were numbered, agreed quite readily, as did John Lever. By his reaction, I gathered John had suspected that something was in the air and was not at all surprised to be approached – he did, however, express surprise that I had committed myself to the trip as he felt more confident of my Test future than I did myself. For him, he said, it was a bonus at the end of an England career; being 33 at the time and never entirely established in the national team anyway, he felt he had little to lose but that my case was altogether different. He gave me food for thought, not that there was much, by then, that I could do about it.

With two, and possibly three, more players ready to go, the tour was clearly given a green light in South Africa and, unbeknown to us, wheels were put in motion to enlist the sponsorship of the South African Breweries group who already backed the prestigious Currie Cup.

Back in Colombo, it is perfectly possibly that these negotiations were a distraction of some degree as we tackled the seventh and final Test match of our tour. It did not help the tension in the air that two senior officials of the Test and County Cricket Board, Donald Carr and George Mann, had arrived to watch the Test. It was rather like having the headmaster watching over you when you planned to slip away early from school, and it led to a good deal of ducking and diving as the principal characters of the project attempted to do their talking away from prying eyes and flapping ears.

I would strongly deny, however, that these dealings in any way detracted from our efforts to beat Sri Lanka. Everyone approached that match in a professional, responsible way and the fact that we rallied so well from a very hazardous position to actually win the game, giving 'Fletch' his first and only win as England captain, surely provides ample testimony to our attitude. Midway through the game, vice-captain Bob Willis delivered a long and loud lecture designed to ensure everyone took the field fully motivated, and I don't think it went to waste. 'Embers' turned the game with a spell of five wickets for five runs just when Sri Lanka – 160 on, seven wickets standing – looked to be in a powerful position on a pitch taking increasing spin. From the threat of defeat we were suddenly in complete control and, with Tavaré making 85 and sharing steady stands with David Gower and myself, we won by seven wickets with a day to spare.

Strange though it may seem, it never occurred to me at the time that this was to be my last Test match, my last England innings, for a period of years. The thought that I could be banned for what I was about to enter into was still no more prominent than a vague and almost unthinkable contingency hovering far back in my mind. I was pleased to have won, delighted for 'Fletch', and by now quite excited – if a shade apprehensive – about what lay ahead. I had still failed to convince Brenda that it was the right thing for me to do, but her protests were muted by a desire to support whatever decision I made. I knew the cricket authorities would not view it in quite the same generous light but convinced myself that I was doing nothing wrong, in fact doing no more than accepting an opportunity to earn a living in much the same manner as someone in any other walk of life would be expected to do.

The tour party arrived home at Gatwick Airport on the morning of Wednesday, 24 February and I, along with Messrs Lever, Emburey and Underwood, went directly to one of the airport hotels for a pre-arranged meeting with Peter Cooke and a solicitor named Leon Seligson. Even this necessitated a deception of a sort, as my parents had driven to the airport to meet Brenda and I. It did not seem the time or place to launch into an explanation of my plans, so I said merely that I had to attend an important meeting and, I'm afraid, kept them waiting for about an hour. In a private room at the hotel, we were told that the plan was to fly to Johannesburg on Sunday, and that the first match was likely to be on 3 March, just seven days away. So far as was known at that stage, there had been no leaks but we were all told once again that we should tell nobody outside our immediate family where we were going or why.

Contracts were produced by Leon Seligson and Peter Cooke warned that they were binding. When World Series Cricket was launched by Kerry Packer, at least two players – Jeff Thomson and Alvin Kallicharran – signed contracts, then changed their minds and were allowed to withdraw without argument. Peter insisted that in this instance no one could pull out once they had signed up. I did not resent him making this plain, in fact I appreciated it, but I still wanted time to show the contract to my own advisors and I asked to take it away with me for 24 hours. I agreed to return to London the following day and bring my own solicitor and accountant to go through the contract. A time was arranged for the meeting, which was to take place at the Royal Garden Hotel in Kensington.

I signed up there, on Thursday, 25 February, and gave my full agreement to the conditions. I would not attempt to withdraw and I would not breach the confidential nature of the venture before we left. Then I went home and waited for the phone to ring. It seemed inconceivable that the plans could still be a secret from everyone at Lord's. Discussions had, after all, been going on for more than a year in their various forms, involving a large number of people, some of whom had already withdrawn. Yet no one had spilled the beans.

I only later discovered that at least two players, John Emburey and Bob Willis, had been contacted by Donald Carr. If the cat was not quite out of the bag, at least its head was showing. Word had somehow reached Lord's that a tour was planned but they were light on details. They did not know when it was due to leave or the names of the players involved, and they did not find out until it was too late. Peter Cooke knew of the leak and brought forward our departure by 24 hours to counter it. He phoned on the Friday to inform me of the new arrangements and I was anything but pleased. After four months in foreign parts, every hour at home was precious, but I could see the logic behind the change and agreed to it. Before I left, however, there were certain things I had to do.

The first of these was to tell my parents. Not only were they entitled to know, they were entitled to hear it from me, and I did not like the idea of them finding out by switching on their television set or picking up the morning paper, particularly as I was not sure how the media might react to the tour. At first, when I explained, they did not appreciate the full implications of the trip. It was only later, when the matter became public knowledge and the vitriol flowed from mouths and pens, that it hit them. And then it hit them hard. My father, especially, was very upset. He was, if you like, a victim of the power of the press, something in which I had never entirely believed until then. He believed everything he read in the papers about me, believed that I was breaking up Test cricket for the sake of a good payday, and he could not understand why I had done it. He even thought I was ruining the good name of his family and he told me so when I came home at the end of the trip. I have never seen him so visibly upset by anything I have done and, even when I explained the full story and gave my side of things, he plainly found it very hard to accept. In the months and years which followed, he has come to see the affair in a different light, but when, during the first winter of my ban, *The Sun* printed an 'exclusive' claiming I had told their reporter Ian Todd that I didn't care about England any more, Dad wrote to me in South Africa, enclosing a copy of the article and anxiously asking why I had said such things.

The fact is I had not said anything remotely similar to what was printed. The quotes were a complete fabrication and I was incensed, not just by the fact that a paper had used such an invented and potentially damaging story, but even more by the anguish it had clearly caused Dad. He has always been a staunch supporter throughout my cricket career, following Essex and England around the country, enjoying the atmosphere and relishing my successes. Now he was being told by a newspaper he had no reason to distrust that his son had no feelings for his country and was perfectly happy helping the South Africans. A cricketer has to come to terms with the media. He has to accept that some good things and some bad things will be written about him, sometimes turn the other cheek and ignore stories which are either unfair or untrue. In the normal course of events I might have done no more than complain to the paper concerned about this story, but after receiving that letter from Dad I decided to sue them., The case, which came to court in the summer of 1984, cost *The Sun* £25,000 and, I hope, put my father's mind at rest.

As I waited, a shade nervously, for the time to depart to South Africa, however, the other matter I had to deal with concerned my county. I felt an obligation to inform them of my involvement, partly because of the wording in my county contract but chiefly through a sense of loyalty. I could not see that the trip was in any way harming to Essex, but I wrote a letter, addressed to secretary Peter Edwards, telling them the nature of the private tour and confirming that I would be returning to report for pre-season training, on schedule, at the beginning of April. I posted the letter on my way to London on Saturday morning. It was, of course, much too late for them to try to stop me going even if they felt inclined, but I had at least made a gesture.

It was arranged that the party would gather for lunch in the Royal Garden Hotel before going to Heathrow. Dennis Amiss was another addition to the squad and I greeted him at the hotel, along with Underwood, Lever, Emburey, Knott and, of course, Boycott, who I was meeting for the first time since his highly controversial departure from India. Peter Cooke told us that Willey, Larkins and Hendrick were due to follow us out the next day and that Old and another addition, Leicestershire's Les Taylor, were already in South Africa, where they had been playing throughout the winter. He was still awaiting a final decision from Geoff Cook, though remained hopeful, and his face betrayed the relief he must have felt that we had all turned up. Peter's phone bill over the previous few days must have been astronomical as he made several routine check calls to each player and was no doubt in regular touch with South Africa. Now he was seeing the rewards of his organization gathered before him.

But there was, though, one blow. A bombshell, in fact, because Bob Willis had changed his mind at the eleventh hour and would not now be coming with us. As England's vice-captain for the previous few years, and as a bowler of vast experience, great achievements and no little charisma, Bob had been considered by the organizers as a prestigious part of the team. In fact, I have no doubt he would have been nominated captain if he had carried through his intention to tour. He has always been held in high esteem by fellow England players and had been an able and often inspiring lieutenant to a number of captains. His name was well known and respected around the cricket globe and his presence would have been good for the image of the team and the success of the tour. His absence simply made things harder for those of us who were going, heaping extra pressure on the established England players amongst us, whose numbers were dwindling fast.

I was surprised at Bob. I had the impression that he felt he was very close to the end of what had been a marvellous England career and that this trip would provide some unexpected icing on the cake. When others had pulled out, he had given no hint that he might follow suit and, even though he was absent from the hotel meeting we had at Gatwick on arrival back from Sri Lanka, I remained convinced that he would be with us.

Maybe he just came around to the conclusion that he would be prematurely ending his international playing career if he went and that, after all, he might still have more to offer and more to gain. If that was the reason, he was so very right. It is another of the great ironies of this tale that, within a matter of three months, England's selectors had decided for reasons known only to themselves that their captain should be sacked.

Keith Fletcher, who was totally innocent and uninvolved during the planning of the South African tour and was later to turn down a small fortune in order to stay loyal to the men who gave him his job, was ditched. Bob Willis, involved in the initial discussions and, I had always thought, a probable starter for the tour until the final few hours before departure, was named to take over. Even leaving aside cricketing and tactical considerations, it seems to me there was a complete absence of logic in that decision.

His withdrawal came too late to make any material difference to the rest of us. Contracts were signed and sealed. There was no turning back now and, to be honest, I don't think any of us even considered trying. Sure, there was a good deal of apprehension, a certain amount of nervous joking and a constant feeling of stepping into uncharted waters. But, by now, everyone in the group had come to a decision for his own personal reasons.

There were, of course, a number of players there whose Test days had gone or were fading fast – Knott, Amiss, Underwood, Old, Hendrick and even Boycott; another group who had not quite managed to hold down a regular place and possibly despaired of ever doing so – Willey, Larkins and Lever. Of the committed players that only left Les Taylor, the one uncapped player in the party, John Emburey and myself, and in the weeks and months which followed it was the three of us who were regularly portrayed as having had the most to lose by our decisions.

On that chilly, penultimate day of February, however, all that concerned us was effecting our exodus to Johannesburg without arousing any further suspicion, so, after a good lunch and a general chat, the seven players plus solicitor Leon Seligson boarded a full-size luxury coach, just one of the little extravagances which were about to be heaped upon us. At Heathrow, where we were booked on the six o'clock evening flight to Johannesburg, we all walked through the airport terminal as individuals, checking in and passing through customs never less than 50 yards apart. It was probably an unnecessary precaution, but none of us wanted any hassle, at least until we were safely in South Africa, and, whether or not the exaggerated caution had anything to do with it, we were not spotted and there did not seem to be an inquisitive journalist in sight.

Flying can very often be boring, a test of patience and endurance. But not this flight. No expense and no effort had been spared to make sure we felt welcome, and the effect was certainly achieved. Our seats were in the exclusive upstairs deck of a jumbo jet, first-class tickets and five-star treatment. The champagne which we were constantly offered, the exotic food served and the general quality of service and comfort might be familiar to many a highly-paid business executive on expense accounts, but international cricketers are used to travelling economy class, with all its attendant aggravations. By comparison, this was like stepping out of a clapped-out Mini into a new Rolls-Royce, and I think we all touched down in Johannesburg feeling well fed and watered and generally quite content with life.

We were pretty soon brought down to earth in more ways than one. As soon as we stepped out into the arrivals hall at the airport, where Joe Pamensky and Ali Bacher of the South African Cricket Union were waiting to greet us, we were whisked away into a private room, plainly pre-arranged by our new sponsors, and told what was expected of us, beginning with a major press conference for radio, television and newspapers that same Sunday evening.

Cars drove us into the city, to the Balalika Hotel, our base for just one night before we were moved into the Rosebank for the duration of our stay. My first thought on settling into my room was to phone Brenda, but the call only served to depress and deflate me. She told me that, already, she felt under severe pressure, that Doug Insole – vice-chairman of Essex and a leading figure within the Test and County Cricket Board – had phoned and virtually demanded to know what I was doing and why, and that the reaction in England was building up into something hostile. We were being called rebels and mercenaries and it hurt her. She had never changed her mind about the trip and still felt I should not have gone. Now she was at home suffering the consequences alone, and quite audibly felt pretty miserable about it.

I now knew that we were letting ourselves in for something probably bigger than any of us had bargained for. The fun had not even begun.

3

Into the unknown

Mrs Thatcher was said to be 'dismayed'. The Sports Minister Neil McFarlane accused us of 'deception'. Virtually everyone labelled us 'The Dirty Dozen'. And these were among the milder reactions to our arrival in South Africa.

So great was the furore which exploded about us that Ali Bacher, the former South African captain and leading campaigner for a renewal of international sport with his country, confessed to the press that there was still a chance the whole thing could be called off. I was very relieved that that never happened. We had all suffered plenty of tension during the build-up to the trip and to have it abruptly cancelled when we were actually ready and waiting to play in South Africa would have been like an actor finding himself naked on stage before a first-night full house.

I was also gratified to hear and read some comments which were not against us. The South African press, naturally enough, were all in favour of the visit and we were treated like war heroes at that opening press conference in the Balalika and throughout our stay thereafter. But also, filtering back from London, were some encouraging noises and some supportive cuttings which helped us through a very difficult period.

It came as something of a shock to hear that the matter had caused uproar in the House of Commons, with both Michael Foot and David Steel apparently challenging the Prime Minister to publicly condemn our actions. This she evidently refused to do, confining her remarks in the House to a reiteration of Government backing for the Gleneagles agreement which discourages representative sporting links with South Africa. I understand that there was a good deal of the pantomime-style heckling and shouting which so often decorates Question Time in the Commons and that, all in all, feelings seemed to be running rather high over our expedition.

Much less surprising was the opposition expressed by cricket authorities both in England and the black Test-playing countries. We could hardly have hoped for anything else, although to my way of thinking the allegations that our actions had deliberately and directly put the entire future of Test cricket at risk were hysterical, while the calls from various quarters to ban us all for life from Test *and* county cricket were simply astonishing.

This, however, was still something to be faced in the future. On that opening night in Johannesburg nothing seemed to matter to anyone except that we were there. To the South Africans, starved for longer than even they can have feared of international cricket, constantly buoyed up by false hopes and then mentally bruised and deflated when the door was once again slammed in their faces, this was the realization of a dream. They made us feel important but I don't think any of us could properly have appreciated quite how important we really were in their eyes.

The immediate exposure to the media caught us off guard. We had spent so many months trying to keep the tour plans away from inquisitive journalists that it seemed hopelessly incongruous to now be stood up before them all and expected to explain our every move. The press were gathered in a room at the hotel, apparently knowing only that the South African Cricket Union were about to make a major announcement. Joe Pamensky and his fellow officials went in to address the conference and we were then formally announced and wheeled in to stand or sit behind a table. Speaking for myself, and probably for the others too, I felt very self-conscious. I am not fond of these manufactured press conferences at the best of times and this one seemed especially artifical. Cameras inevitably flashed and snapped and the picture of the seven of us, wearing a variety of sports shirts and sipping water poured out by a bearded Geoffrey Boycott, was wired off to London and used in virtually every English national paper the following morning. Questions were fired at us from around the room but our answers were neither revealing nor controversial. They were never likely to be as, with the best will in the world, there was little we could tell anyone at that stage. We were not even sure who would be playing for us, let alone against whom we would be playing and when.

These were the problems which occupied us for the rest of Sunday evening. Twelve players had so far been contracted, which was not sufficient for the type of hectic schedule we were now warned to expect. We were at least a batsman short and the priority was to determine whether Geoff Cook would be joining us. Frankly, I believed he would, as he had seemed quite keen on the idea when we put it to him in Colombo. But either second thoughts on his own behalf, or a persuasive argument on someone else's, had changed his mind. Geoff Boycott got through to his home in Northampton and Cookie was quite adament that he would not be joining us. This was quite a disappointment as we had considered Cook would be the ideal man, both as a cricketer and a personality, to complete our party. He had never quite made it as a regular England player but he was technically excellent against fast bowling, of which we expected to face plenty, and had the sort of easy-going good humour which is valuable to any touring team.

So now we had to think again and it did not take long to come up with the name of Keith Fletcher. By now he was bound to be aware of what had happened, probably even feeling sore that it had gone on behind his back, but now that he had completed his duties as tour captain there seemed no reason why we should not give him the opportunity to make up his own mind about his future. It was decided that I should phone him, as a county team-mate, and it felt rather odd when I got through to him in his delightful rural home. I didn't doubt that he had spent the day pottering in his beloved garden or maybe shooting or fishing, his other main hobbies, and I wondered if he had expected a call when he heard the news of our departure. I put the proposition to him – he would be paid a fee of £45,000 and he would be back home in good time for the start of Essex's pre-season training programme at the beginning of April. 'Fletch' said he felt unable to decide on such a major issue on the spur of the moment and asked for 24 hours to make up his mind. This was no more than reasonable, in the circumstances, but I always had the feeling that Keith would be reluctant to put the England captaincy at risk, even for such a sum of money. I was right. When he phoned back as arranged, and spoke to Peter Cooke it was to give his regrets and his refusal. Much later, I think he had cause to regret that phone call.

Fletcher's decision meant that we were not just a player short, but a captain short, too. Willis, as I have said, was the natural first choice for the post. With him discounted, the job would have gone to 'Fletch' if he had come. Peter Cooke now consulted the players on who should be appointed and, I think, got a clear message that Boycott would be a controversial choice. We all had too much on our plate to say anything more to the man about his exit from India, but words were not necessary; feelings still ran deep, the incident had not been entirely forgotten or forgiven and to accept Boycott as leader would have been illogical. Alan Knott was mentioned as a candidate, but he has never been keen to captain. 'Knotty' is a singular, idiosyncratic cricketer, brilliant at what he does but frequently difficult for other players to relate to.

All of which conspired to leave me with the job. I had no experience of leadership and it was not pre-ordained that I would be captain, as many people seem to have assumed. In fact, it had not even occurred to me until we had been in South Africa for a day or more that there was any chance of it. It did not seem to me to be of major importance and, although I was naturally pleased that the other players thought enough of me to put me at the top of the list, I can't say I considered it an honour in the way that captaining England or even Essex would be.

In hindsight, I may have been wrong to accept. Certainly, I had misjudged the interpretation that the press and public would place upon the appointment. I had, rather thoughtlessly, assumed that I would be considered a figurehead captain, elected from the ranks, and that, apart from skippering the side on the field and conducting the occasional routine press conference, my part in the tour would not be thought markedly different to that of anyone else. Instead, as I was rapidly to discover, the captaincy meant that I would never again be thought of as 'just one of the crowd in South Africa'. From the moment that I took the job and the announcement was made to the press, both South African writers and the English contingent who had begun to arrive in what seemed like plane-loads, my name was synonymous with the tour and the pressure on me and my wife doubled. The party was no longer referred to as merely a team of English players, or even as 'The Dirty Dozen'. From then on, we were 'Gooch's Rebels', and that was something I could never grow to like.

The extent to which the media labels, linking me with the trip in every story, had permeated the public thinking, did not get through to me until I returned to England. Then, in conversation with anyone from close friends and family to complete strangers, I was made uncomfortably aware of how it was imagined I must have been behind the whole thing. I was singled out from the group and I think some people, given the chance, would have proposed double the punishment for me as captain.

Once incident in particular drummed this home. In May of that year, back home in Essex, I was playing in a benefit match for 'Fletch'. The venue is unimportant, as is the identity of the people involved. It was a club ground and I was signing the steady stream of autograph books which are customarily pushed the way of all the players on these occasions. One small boy, who cannot have been older than six, came up with his father, who said to him: 'That's Graham Gooch.' The boy replied: 'Isn't he the one who is a traitor?' It seemed funny at the time and I certainly didn't add to the father's embarrassment, but it was another instance to show just how much influence the newspapers have over everyone.

At the same time that the captaincy was resolved, a tour committee was also appointed, which would be responsible for selecting the teams and conducting all the necessary negotiations with the SACU. Peter Cooke, whom by now I had come to like and respect, had a place on this as manager and there were three players involved – Boycott, Emburey and myself.

Our first task was to agree on an itinerary, which proved to be more difficult than I had anticipated. The SACU, having got their men, did not intend to let us imagine we were on holiday. In the space of less than a month, they insisted on cramming in three four-day matches against the full South African XI – which, by now, we knew for certain would be billed locally as 'Test matches' – and three one-day matches, also against the full South African side. This was fair enough, but we insisted on a certain number of practice matches, as a proportion of our party had played no cricket since the previous September and it was asking too much of them to go straight into an important match.

Joe Pamensky and Ali Bacher were not prepared to budge from the quota of showpiece matches they had clearly planned between themselves and by the time the required number of warm-up games and provincial matches had been accommodated our schedule looked hopelessly crowded. With a day allowed for travelling between matches, we did not have a completely free day for four weeks. Most of us considered this to be a harsh demand, but personally I was well aware that we were not in a great position to bargain. We were being paid handsomely, and that is an understatement. I do not intend to spell out here the precise figure that I, or anyone else, received for our services, but it was several times greater than any of us have ever been paid for an England tour lasting more than three times as long. That, I think, puts the matter into perspective and was the one unarguable reason why we were unable to dictate how many games we were prepared to play.

Boycott, however, took a less equivocal line. Throughout our stay it was evident that he did not see eye to eye with Bacher on anything at all, a personality clash which may well have dated back a number of years, and Geoffrey felt so strongly that we were being asked to play too much that he got up and walked out of one meeting with the SACU men. It was not an exhibitionist exit – he just picked up the notebook in which he constantly records his thoughts and marched silently from the room, several pairs of eyes following him in astonishment.

To be fair to Geoff, this was an isolated instance of the sort of behaviour many people imagine he indulges in constantly. He was in his element in South Africa, where he had plenty of friends, a great deal of contacts and – important to him – a true liking for the country.

Over the years there has invariably been a simmering feud between 'Fiery', as he is euphemistically known, and either individuals in a team or the whole side. The situation at Yorkshire is just one example of this; with England things have often been equally bad.

It is things like this which have won Geoff Boycott a reputation as an awkard customer. He has it in him to be unpleasant to people and he has been accused of being rude on many occasions. I would put this tactlessness down to him being accustomed to getting what he wants and I think he respects those who stand up to him. Let me now make it clear that I feel I get on with Geoff better than most. He is, for better or worse, a respecter of ability and because he happens to think I am somewhere approaching his standard as a batsman he probably has more time for me that he would for a player he considers his inferior. To my knowledge, he does not have many of what I would call very good friends among contemporary cricketers but, having said that, he has plenty of staunch friends and supporters outside the playing ranks, as recent events within his county have proved.

He could sometimes be thought difficult to understand on the field as well as off. Here, however, I think he is misunderstood. His running, for instance, is always being heavily criticised but I happen to think he is good between the wickets and that so long as his partner calls loud and early he will respond. He is involved in run-outs with a certain monotony but that is partly because singles are an ever-increasing part of his game. Years ago, he hit a relatively high proportion of boundaries but the older he has got the more introspective his batting has become; singles are one way in which he can keep the score moving, so he seeks them out in great numbers rather than resort to aggression.

Boycott's cricketing brain is finely-tuned and I would always turn to him for tactical advice. His personality, however, is so single-minded that it gives him the image of a recluse. I have never known a cricketer to be seen so seldom, especially during lengthy overseas tours. I have never seen him in a hotel bar and he spends most of his free time in his room when he is not in the nets, seldom mixing with team-mates or opposition unless it is an official function. None of this is especially endearing to his fellow players, most of whom would not pretend to understand Geoff, but because he is such a loner he takes very little effort to get along with.

It would have been nothing new to him in South Africa to feel that certain of our players were distant towards him over what had happened in India, and he was thick-skinned enough to cope with it as if the feeling did not exist. He was constructive at committee meetings once the itinerary had finally been agreed, and as intelligently astute as ever when it came to on-field tactics. He did not enjoy an especially successful tour with the bat, but his name was so big there that the crowds were happy to greet him as a hero anyway, and I was certainly glad to have his ability in our team.

Once we knew when and where we were expected to play, we still had to return to the problem of securing reinforcements for our shoestring squad. And so began the saga of the Thirteenth Man, a mystery which the English media evidently delighted in for days. Many possibles were put forward by the press, some of the names wholly fanciful, but we were not prepared to speculate publicly on the identity of any new players until they had actually signed – chiefly for the sake of the individuals concerned. This unintentionally added to the publicity value of what was, nonetheless, a lengthy and complicated tale.

From a room in the Rosebank Hotel we drew up our short list. Top of it was Derek Randall, who had been a controversial omission from the England side to India but, we all knew, would be a great crowd-pleaser if we could get him. Clive Rice, Derek's county captain at Notts and now a key figure in the South African team we were about to face, knew of his whereabouts in Melbourne and offered to phone him on our behalf. 'Arkle' – the nickname arising from his galloping gait in the field – dallied a little, but eventually declined. Paul Parker, who had played one Test for England the previous summer but failed to win a place on the winter tour, was the next man we contacted, tracking him down in Western Australia to outline the terms. He, too, said no.

By now we had been in South Africa three days and were into our opening match, a two-day game against a selected under-25 side. And still we had only the bare 12 players. From the ground in Pretoria, after I had been dismissed for 33, I tried to contact Alan and Roland Butcher, both of whom had played for England without establishing themselves, but fitted the bill as the top-order batsmen we needed. Both, I was led to believe, were at home in England, but despite trying several times I failed to get through to either of them.

Desperation was beginning to creep in now, as we badly needed to sign someone before going into our second match, a one-day international at Port Elizabeth on the Saturday. It was an odd situation because, in the minds of all the players, there was only one man we really wanted and we happened to know he was available. That was Alvin Kallicharran.

Now, this might sound nonsensical. Kallicharran, after all, is a West Indian – albeit a banned-for-life West Indian. But there was method in the madness. We wanted Alvin for two main reasons – the first being that he was the best available player and was readily on hand in South Africa, where he had been playing for Transvaal; the second being that he was patently a non-English player. The South Africans were trying very hard, despite my own stated reservations on the issue, to promote us as an English, if not an England, team. This was understandable from their viewpoint of trying to sell the series to the public and to advertisers at very short notice, but for us it was merely adding to the pressure. We did not see ourselves as representing our country, so the presence of Kallicharran would have been beneficial in more than one, obvious sense.

Now that we knew for sure we would be playing the equivalent of South Africa's Test team, at full strength and in practice, it was doubly important for us to have the best man available. Alvin had indicated that he would be keen to play and so we pressed his case, justifying it with the sceptical SACU officials by pushing the fact that he was a long-standing county player who had lived in England for many years. I could tell that they were unconvinced by our arguments but when, on the Friday journey to Port Elizabeth, I met Geoff Dakin, second-in-command to Joe Pamensky, I tried again to persuade him of Kalli's value. Mr Dakin has a loud and somewhat unsubtle voice and he proceeded to use it in an airport lounge full of wagging ears to promise that we could have Kallicharran 'if we were unable to get anyone else'.

This promise never needed fulfilling because we could get someone else, not in the same class and very definitely English, but also on the spot and available. Geoff Humpage was our thirteenth man and I have no doubt the announcement was seen in England as a complete anti-climax. Humpage had not played in a Test, nor probably been seriously considered for one, but he had been chosen for one-day internationals as a hard-hitting batsman who could also keep wicket and it was in this dual role that we saw him being useful. As a pure wicketkeeper he could not even be compared with Alan Knott, but he could command a place in many teams for his batting alone and so we selected him against Western Province, hoping he might create competition in the top order. As things turned out he was not chosen again on the tour and, to his credit, cared enough to come and ask us why he was constantly being overlooked. In his position, no doubt surprised by the offer in the first place, it would have been all too easy to pocket the sizeable cheque and enjoy the holiday but, although we had warned him when he signed that there could be no guarantees over how much he would play, I was impressed by his professional approach.

This was never likely to be the last of our signings. To be honest, Geoff might well not have been contracted at all but for a doubt which existed over the fitness of Bob Woolmer. The Kent player, who has since sadly retired through another, quite unconnected injury, was at the time struggling on a damaged ankle. He had been happy to say yes when we approached him about joining, and he was on the scene in South Africa, where he had been coaching, but there was no prospect of him being fit for the Western Province match and we felt security was needed immediately.

Woolmer did later sign for us, and our fifteenth and final recruit was Arnie Sidebottom, the Yorkshire fast bowler, who had been playing for Orange Free State in the Currie Cup. Injuries had by this time begun to affect our party, Mike Hendrick once again falling victim to the type of niggling problem which has blighted his career, and Arnie was paid on a match-by-match basis. He did play in the two one-day internationals but I wondered if he later considered he might have been unwise to join up for such limited cricket and limited payment. He might well have been an England bowler by now if he had not.

Having a full squad and an agreed itinerary did not, of course, resolve everything. For the first week of the stay, in particular, certain of the players found themselves put under almost intolerable pressure from home, and all of us were under constant, unsettling scrutiny from the legions of pressmen who had arrived on the scene.

The latter contingency came as no surprise. You cannot run a cricket tour to South Africa without exciting media interest, and we had to accept that the journalists had been sent out there as part of their job and were expected to collect as much material as possible – in some cases, by whatever means available. Peter Cooke had warned everyone before they signed that there would be pressure and there would be criticism but that the most he would be able to offer was support and sympathy, certainly not an early flight home for anyone who could not stand the heat.

We could do a certain amount to minimise the problem. Telephonists at all the hotels we used were instructed to identify everyone phoning to speak to any of the players and to connect only family. Press callers were all diverted to Peter Cooke. I handled all the end-of-play press conferences myself on the strictly observed proviso that I would answer any questions on the cricket but none at all on politics. This was plainly an unpopular edict and certain tabloid-newspaper writers were openly resentful about our attitude, while others resorted to waving chequebooks under the noses of our players in an effort to prise some sensational quotes from their reluctant mouths. No one wavered from our agreement, however, and I believe none of the players disclosed the full details of the tour to a newspaper.

It could be claimed that we were being unreasonably reticent with the press but I maintained that the tactics were justified. We were all professional sportsmen, there to make a living, but we may well have had diverse political views about South Africa. For individuals to have expressed those views and attracted even more controversy would only have been creating trouble for ourselves.

The journalists, however, would doubtless have claimed they were under just as much pressure as us through being expected by their offices back home to justify the considerable expense of their trip with one or two meaty stories. So they persisted manfully. Some of them, indeed probably most of them, had come to write of the political aspect rather than the cricket and the fact that we would not give individual interviews did not prevent them operating. When we phoned home, as most of us did each evening during that first week, our wives would tell us what had appeared in the English papers. Little of it was designed to cheer us up or view the attendant writers in a kindlier light.

No sportsman can expect immunity from the power of the pen, nor should anyone be resentful about justifable criticism or an honestly expressed opinion. But it does seem to me that tabloid papers in England have reached a stage where sportsmen must either be painted as heroes or villains. There is no grey area in between, and the extremes can often be cruelly applied. What most annoyed me was that writers whom I happened to know had described us as being very close to the criminal class would still approach, wreathed in smiles and bonhomie, to ask for an exclusive interview, and then be surprised and offended when you refused.

All of us, however, probably remember the bad things written about us and forget too easily the good things. I can relate it to batting, where I am much more likely to carry the memory of a bad umpiring decision which cost me my wicket than an equally bad one which spared me. And there were some good, by which I mean favourable, articles written about the venture, not to mention a stack of letters written to newspapers expressing support for what we had done. On 4 March, the second day of our opening game, *The Daily Telegraph* printed eight letters on the issue, all of them in our favour. One said that the outrage being expressed was 'hypocritical in the extreme' and went on: 'Quite apart from the fact that South Africans, West Indians, Indians and Pakistanis play freely together in our county programme, businessmen of all nationalities visit South Africa daily in furtherance of their commercial interests. So why not cricketers, as do already golfers, tennis players and so on?' Another asked: 'Why is it so dreadful to play cricket against South Africa, when we are quite happy to play Russia at football, even after Afghanistan?' And a third pointed out: 'Our supermarkets are full of tinned goods imported from South Africa. Is it not hypocrisy to ban sports between the two countries and yet import these foods?'

In the months leading up to the tour, during the long days and endless evenings in rural India, I had had plenty of time to consider all the implications of what I was doing, and every one of these points had entered my head at some stage. I was sure there were hypocrisies. I could not understand why cricketers should be singled out for the rough treatment. And these convictions helped sway me towards the decision I eventually made.

There were times, in the troubled course of our early days in South Africa, when I wondered if I had been a fool to myself. But I came to realize that this was prompted by personal martyrdom and by concern for Brenda left at home. When she, and the rest of the wives, arrived at the end of the first week, every player was happier and more settled, even if the problems did continue to pile up for us.

4

Three years

A phone call can be a trap for pent-up emotions. Speak in haste, repent at leisure. I found that out the hard way.

Mere separation can put a strain on a relationship, as many married couples discover each year. But for Brenda and I, not simply apart but both under unusual pressures, the first week of March 1982 was among the most difficult we have been through. We argued down a long-distance phone line, which is never a good idea.

Brenda, as I have said, had never made any secret of her attitude towards my touring South Africa. She thought I was making a mistake and she told me so, but having done that she was far too loyal to put any barriers in my path. Had she known what she would have to go through during my absence, however, she just might have voiced her objections more strongly.

We were wrong, looking back on it, to have left our wives at home when we made our undercover flight to Johannesburg. To have taken them would certainly have made it more difficult to maintain the element of secrecy, but in a sense we were abandoning them to face the worst of the reaction. If not exactly immune from it ourselves, we were at least living a protected existence in South Africa, moving everywhere as a group and spending most of our waking hours in hotel rooms or at cricket grounds with our phone calls screened and the fury of the men at Lord's purely a matter for our imagination. Our wives were isolated and vulnerable back in England.

Brenda's opposition to the trip hardened during our week apart. We spoke on the phone every evening but eventually the calls were neither a relief nor a pleasure. Both of us were tense and when that happens it is all too easy to say rash, unwise things into the anonymity of a telephone.

One evening we began to quarrel again over the merits of the tour and why I was there. It was by now a familiar dialogue and one which was leading us nowhere. 'Come on,' I snapped. 'Make up your mind. You're either with me or you're against me.'

That was enough to terminate the conversation pretty rapidly and to leave us both feeling miserable for the next 24 hours. But Brenda had every right to be on edge. Ever since I had left on the Saturday morning, she had been bombarded with telephone calls. They came from cricket officials, newspapermen, family and friends, and they all wanted to know what I was doing and why. Some of the callers, especially the press, made her feel I had committed some dreadful crime against the country. More than once, they reduced her to tears. At least one newspaper sent writer and photographer to our front door.

I know she was pressured by a member of the cricketing establishment – not, I am sure, acting on any agreed line but as an individual phoning up to tell her I should not have gone. As she already privately agreed with him, this only made things even harder for her. I know she was not the only wife to suffer in this way and Dennis Amiss, for one, became distressed at the number and the tone of the phone calls his wife Jill was receiving back in Birmingham. Warwickshire, along with Northants, appeared to be leading the revolt against the tour and advocating the strongest line against the players who had gone. (Northants went so far as to announce that we should all be banned for life, including their own Peter Willey and Wayne Larkins and, although later defeated, I think this proposal had a lot to do with the rift which led to Willey leaving the county.)

Brenda's closest friend among the other wives was Susie Emburey and during this fraught week they adopted a code. If they phoned each other, they would allow the bell to ring three times, then disconnect and dial again. Brenda tells me that Susie's calls were eventually the only ones she answered other than when I rang at a prearranged time.

She also did something rather strange, something even she is at a loss to explain. Knowing all too well that the papers were crucifying the players in general, and me in particular as captain, she still went every day to our local newsagent, bought a copy of every morning paper and then read and cut out every story relating to the tour. I am sure she was torturing herself more each day, but she persevered with the routine and, when she flew out to join me at the end of the week, she brought with her a large batch of cuttings, most of which gave me no pleasure at all. Also in her bag was a bundle of letters which had arrived for me in my absence. Some had already reached me in South Africa too and, while there were naturally some vitriolic attacks on my morals in amongst them, I would estimate that 80 per cent of the mail I received over the entire period was sympathetic and supportive, much of it giving the tour credit for cutting through the hypocrisy surrounding the South African issue.

The flow of mail was to increase substantially when the Test and County Cricket Board carried out their threat and banned us from Test cricket. Hindsight dictates that none of us should have been surprised and yet, without exception, we all were.

People still seem reluctant to believe me when I say I never expected to be banned but I am not going to change my story now, when it happens to be the truth. Sure, I might have been naïve, but I thought back to the attempted ban on the men who joined World Series Cricket, rescinded in some embarrassment and at great cost to cricket after a stormy court case, and I honestly believed the TCCB would be neither wise nor justified in trying the same treatment again. Others in our party took a more cynical view, and admittedly there were those whose career had reached the advanced stage at which they no longer greatly cared about the consequences of the tour.

Once we were in South Africa, none of the players received a single phone call from Lord's attempting to entice us back. But of course we would have been living in a fool's paradise if we had for a moment translated this as meaning our mission was being condoned. It did, however, cross my mind that the men who held our fate in their hands might possibly be thinking the same way as Frank Keating did when he wrote a long piece for his paper, *The Guardian*, on 1 March.

Frank has been a friend for some years. He is a journalist I trust and admire, a man I like enormously. But I knew of his hatred for the South African system and, indeed, had discussed it with him at length, so I was grateful for the balance and the reason behind his writing. After saying 'surely there can be no equivocation from Lord's', he went on to pose the salient question:'What other young married professional man, from accountant to journalist even, has to consider whether to take up a short-contract job in South Africa in the knowledge that all the world's idealogues will heap scorn on his shoulders if he accepts? While acknowledging the evil in South Africa, Gooch's dilemma – and indeed that of all those in the party – is an unfair one on which we should be careful in pious ascent to the pulpit. Why should he, a professional man with a short-term earning capacity, really be expected to feel a sense of guilt that his presence on the field at a whites-only sports club in Johannesburg has anything to do with the lack of sports equipment or multi-racial facilities in Soweto's black township?'

Perhaps there really was such an uncluttered opinion expressed at Lord's but, two days after that article appeared, they fired the first warning shot to us with a written, collective plea to abandon the tour and come home. The board's message read: 'We must make you aware of the very strong reaction in England and other countries to the proposed participation by you and other English cricketers in international calibre matches in South Africa. In particular, the India and Pakistan tours of the United Kingdom this summer could clearly be in danger if the proposed matches take place, thus seriously affecting county finances and the possible future livelihood of fellow cricketers.'

'Indeed, if it is thought practicable for you to do so, we urge you to reconsider your position and refrain from playing in any such matches.'

The letters, which came in the dual names of George Mann and Donald Carr, chairman and secretary of the board, were individually addressed to each of the 12 players signed at that stage and delivered to us via the British Embassy's diplomatic bag. The board's intentions went slightly awry, however, as the letters failed to reach us until our match with the under-25 XI in Pretoria was underway, by which time I imagine the 'crime' had been committed in their eyes.

It would have made no difference, anyway, as I am confident

none of the 12 players would have been swayed towards trying to break their contract. They all read the letter and no one expressed any desire to go home or any regret at the situation in which they found themselves. Of the entire group, I would estimate that only Wayne Larkins might have privately been having second thoughts. Frankly, I think he was more surprised than anyone by the hornet's nest we had disturbed, and particularly stunned by the aggressive response of his own county, which appeared, at that stage, to be threatening him with the sack from his bread-and-butter employment. Peter Willey, his Northants team-mate, was in the same position, but he viewed it all much more contemptuously. I am not convinced that Wayne would have jumped at the chance of a rapid return ticket with no questions asked, but I do think he was unsure whether he had done the right thing.

Of the rest who were likely to be directly affected by a ban from Test cricket, John Emburey was committed to the tour, having made up his mind in India that it was the right thing for him to do, and the uncapped but highly rated Les Taylor had told me several times that it was his firm opinion he would never be chosen for England. His conviction that his colliery background was sure to be held against him could have persuaded him to accept the tour and, although subsequent events suggest he may well have been sacrificing a Test career, it plainly did not bother him at the time.

We were soon made aware that it would not be long before we knew our futures. The TCCB were to discuss the tour at a meeting on 9 March, while we were playing our only three-day warm-up game, against Western Province at Cape Town. The papers, naturally enough, were full of speculation, much of it falling into the 'ban the lot of them for life' category. But among those who put our side of things was the cricket correspondent of *The Times*, John Woodcock. He wrote of 'the hysterical reactions of people who should know better' and went on: 'You would think that Gooch and Emburey, though doing nothing that as citizens of a free country they are not perfectly entitled to do, have disqualified themselves for good and all from playing for England again. For myself I sincerely hope . . . that they will be in Australia later this year, warmly welcomed as members of the England side.'

'As for the chances of this summer's tours of England by India and Pakistan surviving, that must not depend upon the TCCB agreeing to ostracise Gooch and the rest of them. Having done their best to stop them from going to South Africa, the TCCB, as the guardians of English cricketers, should work now to save their England places. As indeed, should the ICC, who came to a unanimous agreement at their last meeting that no one member country should dictate to the selectors of another.'

This gave me cause for optimism, as indeed did a letter in the following day's edition of *The Times* from no less a person than Lord Chalfont. He wrote: 'It is not reasonable, or indeed tolerable, that citizens of this country should be deprived by harassment, blackmail or threat, of their freedom to pursue their sporting activities either for pleasure or for gain, wherever they wish to do so. There is no law in this country, as there is in some others, which forbids travel abroad. United Kingdom citizens are therefore free to go to South Africa whenever they wish, on business or for pleasure.'

'The Government may, in its wisdom, forbid certain categories of commerce or trade for reasons of state; sporting bodies may justifiably decline to allow representative teams to travel under their auspices. *No one* has the right to tell an individual law-abiding British citizen where he may play his games, earn his living or enjoy his leisure.'

So strongly did I support that final sentence that I marked it in blue pen and kept the cutting nearby in my hotel room. It seemed to me, as apparently it did to Lord Chalfont, that the reaction to our going had been full of confusion and hypocrisy. I remained confident that the TCCB would agree.

On the second evening of the game against Western Province, I returned to the De Waal Hotel in Cape Town feeling a shade apprehensive. Brenda was waiting for me in the room and we tuned in the radio to BBC's World Service to listen to the news. We did not have long to wait – it was one of the main items of the bulletin and it struck home like a thunderbolt.

Three years. I could not immediately take it in. Perhaps now I know how a prisoner feels, standing in the dock convinced of his own innocence but hearing the judge pass sentence, sending him to jail. Brenda and I were both shocked into utter silence and for some while we just stared at each other, numbed and miserable. I suppose it would have been easy, given her views throughout the affair, for Brenda to have said 'I told you so', but instead all she did was look just as upset as I felt. Of course, the players had discussed all possible punishments at the meetings we had virtually every evening. The majority were of the opinion that a ban of some sort was likely, but that one year was about the most we could expect. Three years seemed terribly harsh.

When the reasons behind the sentence were explained, of course, it all fell into place. It didn't make it any better but at least I understood. The board's priority had been to save the summer's tours by India and Pakistan, so they made sure we were out of the way for them. Then they looked farther ahead to the next World Cup, scheduled for England in 1983, and doubtless feared that all the non-white countries would withdraw if we were allowed to play in that. Finally, they plainly considered the money-spinning visit by West Indies in 1984 and the tour of India which followed. They decided that we should be disqualified until all of these series had been completed, becoming eligible again – those who were still young enough and fit enough – in time for the home Ashes series with Australia in the summer of 1985.

If Australia had been due to tour England instead of the West Indies in 1984, I am convinced our ban would have been for only two years – and if there had been no World Cup to worry about it might have been one year. So we could probably be considered unlucky, although for George Mann to claim 'it is not a punishment' seemed, from where I stood, absolutely laughable. If it was not a punishment to ban us for three years, I would like to know what he would consider a punishment.

What I think he was accepting without using plain language to say so was that it was perfectly clear to everyone at Lord's that we had not even broken any contracts, let alone broken any laws. We had taken up the right of an Englishman to earn a living where and in whatever legal way he chooses, which is normally one very good reason for being English.

Back in October the TCCB had been fighting to preserve another tour – the England trip to India – in the face of what seemed to me to be the very objections they were now concerned with again. Geoff Boycott and Geoff Cook, for whatever reasons, business or pleasure, had spent some time in South Africa. Cook had played and coached in Eastern Province, Boycott had coached and holidayed in Johannesburg. The Indians objected and retorted with the threat that the England team would not be welcome if it included these two players. Call it a form of political blackmail if you like, but it put the tour in real jeopardy, and tested the principles of the TCCB.

They stood up well and I admired them for their resolve. Refusing to change their selected touring side or in any way to discipline the two players concerned, they merely agreed to a compromise which involved Boycott and Cook stating their abhorrence of apartheid. The tour went on and Boycott was later even able to have a joke over the matter with the Indian Prime Minister Indira Ghandi, when she was introduced to us at Delhi, solemnly presenting her with a copy of his latest book, having underlined a passage in it which confirms his views on South African apartheid. Mrs Ghandi had told him: 'I will accept your book – because you caused me so much trouble before the tour.' All very chummy, and no face lost on either side.

George Mann issued a statement when the issue was resolved which said: 'If we had yielded to the demands to omit Geoff Cook and Geoff Boycott we would have been at the head of a very slippery slope. All cricket boards know where we stand and more governments are realizing that we will not alter our principles of selecting our sides on merit. South Africa found that out 13 years ago, Guyana discovered it last winter and now India's government know where we stand.

I know we had received a warning letter from the TCCB but in my view it is an inescapable fact that they *did* alter their principles. They were no longer going to select their sides on merit. Maybe they had started down that very slippery slope.

Back in Cape Town, however, I had to pull myself together and act the part of a captain. We were only midway through the second week of the trip and, apart from having lost the first of the one-day matches to South Africa, the serious cricket had not even begun.

Although I was completely taken aback by what I had just heard on the radio, any depression had to be nipped in the bud if the tour was not to deteriorate into a shambles. We already had a hard enough job against the best players in South Africa, and the knowledge of what we were going home to was hardly likely to make things any easier. I swiftly called the team together to discuss what had happened.

The reaction of the players was interesting. Everyone knew why the meeting had been called – there had scarcely been an alternative topic of conversation during the day – and as they filed into the appointed room in the hotel, the expressions ranged from the angry to the philosophical. After all that had gone before, we had not tried to kid ourselves too much that the decision would whitewash us completely and yet I do not think anyone had resigned himself to this. It took the course of a nuclear attack. We had had the warning, and we knew something unpleasant was on its way, but we were still completely unprepared for the shock.

We had discussed the legal aspect of the ban in advance and now we were intent on finding out if the TCCB were within their rights to ban us. Obviously, the memory of the Packer case was strong, and four of our players – Knott, Underwood, Woolmer and Amiss – were veterans of that affair too, so no strangers to courtroom procedures. Our first gut feeling was that they could not get away with it. Possibly this was no more than the cry of wounded innocents, and not exactly based on logic, but we did think there was a very good chance that the decision would not stand up in court and the team was unanimously in favour of seeking legal advice. This, however, would have to wait until we returned to England – for one thing, there did not seem much point in spending fortunes on telephone calls to solicitors when we would be home in less than three weeks; for another I wanted to be as sure as possible that the players' minds remained on the cricket rather than being distracted by legal matters.

Pressure from the media was clearly going to step up a gear now but I told everyone I would hold a press conference at which I would simply state the players' general disappointment at the verdict. The rest of the boys were to continue the policy of press silence.

That night, more than at any other time in my life, it was right for me to re-examine my attitude towards apartheid and my opinion of the South African system. For there could be no doubting the fact that I was being penalised because the people of other countries would construe that my actions were directly supporting that system. This was nonsense, of course. I had, and still have, no more sympathy with apartheid than I do with political terrorism or soccer hooligans. Just because I might go to watch a football match does not mean I am championing the cause of the louts – but the parallel was being drawn.

My view of South Africa's policies had not radically altered since I first went there in the winter of 1975–76. I played club cricket for a side called Green Point in Cape Town and made a lot of friends. But while I could be friendly, I could not agree with their political views and social stances. I will forever remember one evening, chatting over a glass of beer at one of the endless barbecues the South Africans put on, a lady who I had met several times before and had grown to like as a person was questioning Brenda and myself about life in London. We were discussing employment, and for some reason the role of the road-sweeper was mentioned. This lady stunned me by saying, quite seriously, 'Don't you have blacks to do that sort of thing?'

The comment was not meant to be malicious. She would not even have appreciated that we felt it was misguided. The Afrikaaner race, I came to see, considered themselves the chosen people and viewed the blacks and coloured who happened to vastly outnumber them in their own land purely as the workers, put there to do the jobs that the master race should not need to stoop to. They see blacks as an entirely different species and cannot see that they should ever be granted equal status. And nor do I think they will ever be convinced otherwise.

Their way of life is totally alien to the way in which I was brought up and the values I was taught to believe in, but when you visit South Africa it can fill you with a sense of futility, because in truth there is very little which can be done to help. The sporting bodies, however, have been trying manfully for many years now to break down the barriers. It would be naïve to believe they have wholly succeeded, because the Government line is still predominant as soon as one leaves the sports ground, but certainly cricket is now multi-racial, almost throughout the country and to a degree which it would be unfair to describe as merely cosmetic.

Those who demand to know why there are no coloured cricketers in the representative South African sides are missing the point. The blacks and the coloureds have no historical background in the game and it is only recently that they have been given a decent standard of coaching and acceptable facilities. Top-class cricketers are not going to emerge overnight and it is wholly understandable that not many blacks or coloureds have yet broken through. But there is an increasing number only just below the highest level. Things have been vastly improved. Cricket clubs are in general completely multi-racial both on and off the field. South African law still, to my knowledge, stipulates that races cannot mix socially in public (although it is permissible at private houses). Green Point, however, openly flouted this law as long ago as 1975 and were one of the first clubs to do so; many more have since followed suit and in my experience it is rare to find a club where all the races are not drinking together in the bar at the end of play.

There is a reversal of apartheid practiced by the South African Cricket Board, the body responsible for the non-white cricket competitions which still exist. They will have absolutely nothing to do with the efforts of the SACU to promote fully multi-racial cricket, their grounds being that 'there can be no normal sport in an abnormal society'. Coloured cricketers who choose to play in the predominantly white leagues have been persecuted by their own kind in an unpleasant situation which reminds me of striking miners attacking their working colleagues. I know of at least one coloured man who plays all his cricket for a Cape Town club under a false name in order to avoid the inevitable, possibly violent, repercussions. I am sure he is not the only one.

The SACB frequently, in my view, do things which can only harm themselves in the long run. In 1983, a friendly but competitive challenge match was arranged between a team of whites, under Chris Cowdrey's captaincy, and a team of coloureds. It was to be played on the ground of a coloured club in Cape Town, but it never took place because growing antipathy by the coloured population made it impossible. Here was a chance for the coloureds to display their cricketing advances against good opposition and no doubt with media interest – yet they simply threw it away.

Late in 1984, I wrote to Hassan Howa, president of the SACB, asking if he would write an article for the benefit brochure I was producing. I had already obtained a piece from Joe Pamensky on behalf of the SACU and I thought it was fair and proper to balance it by giving Mr Howa his say. I told him that his article would be printed as written and I would have published his views no matter how critical they may have been of the Union or of my own visits to the country. But I never so much as received the courtesy of a reply.

South Africa's non-white races are anything but harmonious – the Indians, Africans and coloureds are invariably at odds with each other – but under the umbrella of the SACB their cricketers were told they should disapprove of the tour by an English team. This I found extremely difficult to fathom as, for some years past, county cricketers have been spending their winters in South Africa, many of them employed to go to the coloured clubs and schools and coach them to a level they could otherwise never have hoped to attain.

It would be wrong to pretend that our tour was aimed wholly at the non-white community, however. Wrong, too, to claim that we did as much as we would have liked to for the poor blacks and coloureds while we were there. It would have been educational for us, and valuable for them, if we had been able to spend a day or more in the townships, or even in one of the black homelands, perhaps holding a coaching session so that they could see our goodwill for themselves. But the schedule simply did not allow for it. There just wasn't time.

I still feel, though, that the tour did nobody in South Africa any harm. Quite the reverse. The whites in South Africa are extremely insecure and I would like to feel that out visit – the first for 15 years by an overseas cricket team of any stature – helped show people there is nothing to fear from the outside world. I can understand the protective instincts of the white South Africans rebelling against change. To suddenly hand over control to the blacks would create a situation of pure farce and the whites, despite being the minority race, are naturally reluctant to surrender what they have got. They need to be coaxed into slow change and it is my view that a resumption of international sporting relations, on the basis that those changes will continue, can only be a good thing for South Africa and the rest of the world.

Whether the complicated mix of colour and cultures in South Africa can ever live happily together still strikes me as doubtful. I had only to look around the grounds we played on during our tour to see the entrenched attitudes which all the efforts of sporting bodies have not even begun to break down. The grounds were open in all parts to all races, there was no question of segregation. Yet the different races still congregate in the special areas they always used when things were different – at Newlands, for instance, the coloureds gather in a part of the ground known as The Willows. They have always sat there and they see no reason to change just because they are allowed to.

Probably this is no different to the West Indian crowd at the Oval insisting on their 'pitch' by the old scoreboard even when it had a new press box built upon it or, even, to my Dad and I standing in exactly the same place on the terraces at West Ham every time he took me as a boy. But I am not sure it is good for South Africa's future, all the same.

5
Up against it

No cricketer can be completely at his best when his whole life is being reshaped, out of his control many hundreds of miles away. So it would be foolish to claim we were unaffected by the ban from Test cricket. It did not improve the tour one bit – but equally, it was not the reason we were beaten.

We could claim other extenuating circumstances. Lack of match practice plainly told on certain of our players – Wayne Larkins, for instance, did not find his touch until the trip was all but over – and a couple of injuries took their toll in exposing our limited reserve strength. Mike Hendrick played only the first and last of the first-class matches, missing out when his economical and skilful seam bowling would have been invaluable. Worse still, John Emburey played in none of the four-day international games after breaking a finger against Western Province. He stayed on in a supervisory capacity, but I know his disappointment in being unable to play matched ours in losing one of the world's foremost spinners.

The simplest and most accurate explanation for the outcome on the field, however, is that the South Africans were a superior side. Passing years had left their mark and I don't doubt that the Springbok side of eight to ten years earlier would have been still more formidable, but the 1982 vintage would not suffer by comparison with almost every national team currently playing Test cricket. I discount West Indies who, at full strength, have annihilated everyone in recent years and would conceivably do the same to the present South African team, but I believe the Springboks would have beaten the best England could have put out – in other words a combination of the players on our tour and those who turned it down.

In the acrimonious aftermath, people in England were all too willing to scoff unfairly at the strength of our side. Many times, I read or heard that no more than two or three of the team would have commanded a place in a fully representative England selection, an assessment that I consider was based in some cases on a biased reluctance to face facts. Following the relatively barren period which England has since suffered, I detect far more readiness to point out the dramatic effect the ban did have – the absence, for instance, of three of the most consistent, economical seam bowlers in the country in Lever, Old and Hendrick, of the best wicketkeeper/batsman in Knott and of no fewer than five potential Test openers in Boycott, Larkins, Woolmer, Amiss and myself. Virtually all of these players must have merited strong consideration for the Test team during their suspension, while Emburey and Underwood would almost certainly have been vying for the position of first-choice spin bowler.

At our best, then, we were not far short of a Test-standard team, and yet we failed to win one of the six matches against South Africa in the schedule. All three of the one-day games went the way of the Springboks, two of them comfortably and the last on faster run-rate, and after losing the first of the four-day matches, we drew the remaining two.

Given our shortage of preparation I thought we were far from disgraced by a team containing some still legendary names. The South African batting order was led off by Barry Richards, who needs no introduction, and Jimmy Cook, virtually unknown in England but undoubtedly one of the most effective openers in the modern game. The middle-order was potentially devastating. Peter Kirsten batted at number three, and everyone in county cricket knows what a marvellous player he can be. Graeme Pollock was at four, and surely everyone in the world knows what a batsman he is. Pollock, at 38, may have lost some of his hunger for success but the power and talent were still in glorious evidence. He had just finished top of the Currie Cup batting averages for the umpteenth occasion and, when he walloped 64 not out on his own home-town ground at Johannesburg in the first of the four-day contests, we feared the worst for our bowlers. To their credit, and the general consternation of the South Africans, that was the only occasion on which Pollock threatened to run amok, and John Lever was particularly delighted to dismiss the great man for nought in the next four-day game.

Pollock was followed in the batting order by two of the great allrounders in world cricket, Clive Rice and Mike Procter. 'Procky' began the tour as Springbok captain, but his suspect knees never allowed him to bowl at any pace and he was eventually and reluctantly forced to withdraw from the series and hand over the captaincy to his old mate and contemporary, Richards. Lower down came one or two names which would not be so familiar to an English audience. Alan Kourie was their first-choice spinner, an orthodox left-armer getting in ahead of the leg-break bowler Denys Hobson. Ray Jennings was a very able wicketkeeper and Adrian Kuiper an allrounder who eventually replaced Procter.

Then came a seam attack which was at worst effective and at best devastating. Garth le Roux and Steve Jefferies are now well known through playing county cricket and both took their share of wickets, but far and away the best of their bowlers was the bald giant who appeared for Middlesex in 1981, Vintcent van der Bijl. As usual, Vince had taken far more wickets than anyone else in the Currie Cup (that year it was 75 to the 52 of second-placed Jefferies) and he quite clearly looked forward to the series against our side as one of the highlights of his tragically limited career.

Heaven knows how many Test match wickets Vince would have taken if he had been allowed the opportunity. I have certainly played against very few better exponents of the seam bowler's art and, with his great height and enormous stamina, he is the type of bowler from whom a batsman can never really escape. He has everything – accuracy, late movement and enough pace to make you hurry. Yet, at the start of our tour, he was also riddled by nerves.

It was a surprise to see this gentle giant, as amiable a character off the field as he is impressive on it, quite so anxious, but there was no escaping the signs. In the opening one-day match, played before a packed crowd of 17,000 at Port Elizabeth, the occasion clearly got to Vince. It was a breakthrough very late in his career, of course. He celebrated his thirty-fourth birthday during the trip and he was planning his retirement in order to go into full-time business. He had probably resigned himself to going through life without representative honours and international challenges and suddenly, at short notice, we arrived. The result was that the great man lost his line and length to a degree I had never seen him suffer before.

He made us suffer for it pretty quickly. At Johannesburg we were facing a mammoth South African first-innings total of 400 for 7 declared, Cook having scored a century, and Vince bowled us out for only 150. From 22 miserly overs he returned figures of five for 25 and if it had not been for an unbeaten 66 by Dennis Amiss, proving to everyone watching that at 38 he could still have been doing a valuable job for England, we would have been completely humiliated. We fared slightly better following on and I scored my second hundred of the trip – but Vince still emerged with another five-wicket haul and the upshot was that the Springboks were left needing a mere 34 to win.

That was not the last time this man with the ungainly, flat-footed run-up dominated us. He was the South Africans' most effective bowler in the two remaining one-day matches and, when the tour ended with a drawn four-day game at Durban in which we were at our most effective, he took five for 97 in our innings total of 311 for eight . . . a truly great cricketer.

I was pleased with our performances in the second and last four-day games, and but for the intervention of bad weather we could have even levelled the series. At Cape Town, most of the first day was lost to rain and there never seemed likely to be a result thereafter, but at Durban we had engineered a dominant position when rain totally washed out the third day. The Kingsmead pitch was green and the toss crucial. I won it and enjoyed seeing Les Taylor and Mike Hendrick run through the Springbok batting. They made only 181 and, with Bob Woolmer making a hundred, we led on first innings by 130, but time ran out on us.

My own form had been good throughout. After a shaky start in India, I had flown home from the England tour full of confidence, and I was able to take that confidence with me to South Africa. I made runs in virtually every game and totalled well over 500 runs on the trip, success which was more important to me than might at first appear likely. The captaincy helped me in that I found it very easy to motivate myself for my batting, something which had in the past proved irritatingly elusive. The fact was I had come to realize that I was being branded the ringleader and I had no wish to take all the flak for the tour and then be called a failure as well as a traitor.

It was also in my long-term interests to impress the South Africans. When I signed a contract binding me to the tour I stipulated that the SACU would have to guarantee some future winter employment for me if, for any reason, I needed it. I am a naturally cautious sort and although privately confident in the belief that I would not be suspended from Test cricket, I was still not prepared to take any risks with my security. Lucrative though the tour undoubtedly was, it represented only very short-term employment and I did not think it wise to stake everything on its chances of escaping sanctions. When the ban was announced I suddenly found myself with three blank winters to fill, and the runs I scored during the tour must have helped create interest in my services. The South African Cricket Union, faithful to their promise, altered the registration rules to permit each of the provinces two overseas players as from the start of the following season's Currie Cup competition and this, not surprisingly, opened the way for a rush of offers to the players on our tour.

Eastern Province, the weakest of the five main provincial sides, were first to approach me, but when Ken Funston, former South African Test player and now the chairman of the Western Province selectors, made a rival offer, there was really no contest in my mind. Brenda and I knew and liked Cape Town and had plenty of friends there. I think it is a nicer place than Port Elizabeth and Western Province are quite evidently the superior team. I agreed to join them on a three-year deal and was delighted when, for their second new overseas player, they later opted for my good friend John Emburey. Things had not gone particularly smoothly for 'Embers'. He was prevented from playing in most of the major games by injury and, when the ban came, he was potentially stranded because he had settled for a straight one-year contract, so it must have been a great relief to him to receive an offer from such a powerful province.

As I had feared they might, the South Africans crowed mercilessly

A century in Madras in January 1982 was the highpoint of a frustrating Indian tour. Soon, everything was going to change for me. *Adrian Murrell/All-Sport*

ABOVE The picture which confirmed to the world that the rumours were all true. Messrs Gooch, Emburey, Amiss, Lever and (front) Knott, Underwood and Boycott were all in South Africa. *Associated Press*
BELOW Facing the music ... South African Cricket Union officials Joe Pamensky (left) and Ali Bacher. *Colorsport*

ABOVE Shock and concern registered on the faces of tour manager Peter Cooke and his assistant Martin Locke as our three-year suspensions are announced. *Colorsport*

BELOW LEFT Batting with the man who lost more than anyone through the tour... Keith Fletcher, who turned down a fortune to stay as England captain only to be sacked for his loyalty. *Adrian Murrell/All-Sport*

BELOW RIGHT Mike Procter tosses the coin on a momentous morning for South African cricket – their international breakthrough had begun. *Associated Press*

ABOVE Months earlier, Geoff Boycott and I had opened for England in India. Now it was for the SAB X1 at The Wanderers, Johannesburg. *Colorsport*
BELOW LEFT Vintcent van der Bijl, who proved beyond doubt during our stay that he rates among the finest seam bowlers of his age. *Colorsport*
BELOW RIGHT A great friend and team-mate, John Emburey. We have known each other since schooldays. *George Herringshaw*

I have said all along that a bonus of the affair was the chance to spend more time with my wife Brenda and daughter Hannah, pictured here in our garden at home. *Adrian Murrell/All-Sport*

The old guard and the new stars of Essex: ABOVE LEFT John Lever, still perhaps the best bowler of his type in England; ABOVE RIGHT Ken McKewan, all grace, timing and runs; BELOW LEFT Derek Pringle, with potential still untapped; BELOW RIGHT Neil Foster, who enjoyed heartache and fantasy all so soon.
Adrian Murrell/All-Sport

ABOVE LEFT Ray East and Norbert Phillip, two 'characters' who helped to earn Essex the JPL trophy in 1981 – a performance which was repeated in 1984. *Adrian Murrell/All-Sport*
ABOVE RIGHT Batting during 1984: my best season to date, one in which Essex achieved the double. *Adrian Murrell/All-Sport* BELOW Proud winners of the 1984 Championship. *John Barker*

Trying a shot; puffing through the exercise routine; wiping away the sweat ... and enjoying a well earned rest. This was the scene for me four days a week last winter as I trained with the footballers of the side I support, West Ham.
Adrian Murrell/All-Sport

about beating us. Not so much the players, who were in the main gracious and friendly, but the spectators and followers. I know they had waited a long time for the chance to beat any overseas opposition and I would not begrudge them their celebrations.

Nobody sets out to lose. Nobody in our team could at any stage have been accused of not trying his best. But it is undeniably true that our incentives were narrow. We were fighting for personal pride, possibly the greatest motivation felt by any professional sportsman.But what else was at stake? Unlike the South Africans, we did not regard the four-day matches as Tests, nor did we consider ourselves to be representing England on the field. Every player was being well paid, no matter what the results of the matches, so there was a definite danger of complacency creeping in. As captain, I was often aware that I had a problem trying to stir the team up to the peak of their ability. No one was viewing this as the type of holiday into which so many private tours deteriorate – the cricket was far too cut-throat and the schedule far too demanding for that even to have been a factor – but if the team played poorly one day I thought it rather incongruous, if not meaningless, to bawl them out as a county captain or a Test captain would probably have done. Had I done so I think it would have been self-defeating.

Considering all the difficulties, all the outside pressures, the players maintained a very healthy spirit. We had an eccentric or two in the party – Geoff Boycott and Alan Knott would not win any prizes for sociability – but their ways were familiar enough to us all for that never to be a problem. The players came to accept their unnatural situation, to get on with playing the games and doing the travelling without complaint, in the knowledge and awareness that few cricketers have ever been rewarded so well for such a short tour.

Socially, we were by no means confined to the hotel, a pleasant change from a number of recent England tours on which players have not moved from base without armed bodyguards and, apart from the official team functions, of which there was at least one everywhere we played, several of us accepted invitations to speak at lunches and dinners, where the audience were always very interested in why we had come, whether we regretted it and what future we saw for South African sport.

When the end of March came round and it was time to go home I could honestly say I had enjoyed the tour; I think, with very few exceptions, that view was shared by the rest of our players. But we all knew that life was unlikely to be a bed of roses back in England, and there were some very natural apprehensions.

We discussed at team meetings the general line we should all take when we reached home and agreed that nothing should materially alter – in other words, that there was little to be gained and potentially a great deal to be lost by talking at any length to the press. Our main concern now in this direction was not so much to preserve our privacy, though that was still a factor, but to avoid in any way detracting from our case if we should eventually decide to challenge the Test match ban in court. We had witnessed enough, over the previous few weeks, of the way in which certain Fleet Street tabloid papers operated to know that the offers of substantial sums of money for exclusive revelations would not cease just because the tour was finishing – in fact, they were likely to increase as soon as we landed in London. But everyone saw the folly in taking that course and there was a unanimous pledge to refuse all offers until the matter was resolved and we could see the future more clearly.

First, we had to get home, and everyone was nervous of that. We had heard there was a threat of political demonstrations at the airport. None of us wanted to walk into that. We knew for a fact that we would be besieged by the press. None of us were very keen on that, either. But there was a limit to what we could do about either prospect, not least because our county contracts insisted that we were all back and ready to report for training on the first day of April. As the last match of the tour did not finish until 29 March that gave us little room for manoeuvre.

Most of us travelled home on the same flight, leaving Johannesburg at six in the evening and arriving home early the next morning. The airline gave us permission to remain on board for half an hour after landing in the somewhat optimistic hope that this may persuade waiting pressmen or activists that we had changed our plans, but in fact when we did get through immigration, baggage collection and customs we were pleasantly surprised. There was a gathering of journalists, of course, and the TV cameras flashed on and the microphones were pressed forward as soon as we appeared, but the majority of the questioning was amiable enough and of the promised pack of angry demonstrators there was thankfully not a sign.

The whole process might have been completed without a hitch but for one man. Most of the TV and radio mikes were pressed under my nose but I think the would-be interviewers would quickly have tired of my monosyllabic answers which told them no more than that we had enjoyed a good tour and refused to touch on the implications, cricketing or political. But out of the corner of my eye I noticed Geoff Boycott and his lady friend, Ann, drawing attention to themselves by covering their faces with coats or newspapers as they hurried towards the exit. This was the worst thing they could have done. Not only was it a completely pointless tactic, as they had been recognized and filmed as soon as they appeared, but it ruined the calm, routine nature we had been trying to put across and suggested to everyone there that we felt we had something to hide.

I had arranged to meet up again with both Boycott and John Emburey in central London, where a meeting had been planned for us at the Rugby Club of London. Our tour organizers had been in touch with Tommy Campbell, coordinator of the Freedom in Sport organization, and the upshot was an invitation to talk over our situation with a view to their supporting us in whatever way they could. Jeff Butterfield, who runs the Rugby Club, is a member of Freedom in Sport and was there to greet us, along with three MPs, who I gathered were all sympathetic to our case and eager to help. John Carlisle, the most easily recognizable of the organization's figures, came along later and, having heard our side of the story, the MPs agreed that there may well be a legal argument against the ban and that we should pursue it through solicitors.

It was an interesting experience for me to hear the views of such men, and to learn the extent of their support for our tour. Freedom in Sport has unfairly been labelled with the image of flag-bearers for white South Africa, which is a misleading oversimplification of their ideals, and in recent times they have made definite efforts to concentrate their publicised campaigns on other countries in order to improve that image. Our circumstances, however, were just the type they relished attacking, and it was through John Carlisle and his friends that we were introduced to Linklaters and Paines, the practice of solicitors who successfully handled the Packer case for the three players directly involved, Tony Greig, John Snow and Mike Procter. At another meeting in London, we gave the solicitors full background to the tour and then left them to obtain further relevant material from everyone involved on both sides of the dispute.

I found it comforting to know that we were in the hands of such people, not only experienced and respected in legal circles but also with a good working knowledge of the law as it relates to cricket and cricketers. I was confident we would receive the correct advice but, in the meantime, there were other areas of my life which needed some urgent attention.

The first and most important of these was to repair my relationship with my father. When I went home to see him, a day or two after arriving back, he made no attempt to disguise his feelings. He had read the papers, listened to the radio, watched television and been led into the popular line. He was shocked by what he read in the papers and, like most people, came to believe it. He went further than that. He believed that I had brought his name, the family name, into disrepute and that I can have had no feelings for English cricket. He was so upset that for a time I wondered if things between us would ever be the same again – if he and my mother would ever again come to watch me play and if they would still give advice when I asked. All kinds of things went through my mind, and it was far from easy to persaude Dad that I had acted in any way responsibly.

Things improved when I was able to tell him the full story, rather than the one-sided versions he had been hearing from some quarters. It still took him some while to agree that some good might, after all, have resulted from the tour. As for Brenda's view, all against the tour for so long, her mind had been altered in the time she spent in South Africa and she had come home happy that what I had done was the best thing that could have happened. It later transpired that she could be with me virtually all the year round, rather than being separated for months at a time during an England tour and, while accepting that she was seeing the thing from an entirely selfish point of view, if it was good for the family then my father could begin to see some good in it too.

Over the years, talking to people without entrenched positions in one camp or another, Dad has formed his own views of the tour rather than being dictated to by the media. Suffice it to say that there are no grudges remaining between us, that he and my mother come to watch me play as frequently as ever.

Essex could have been hostile towards John Lever and myself, but life went on much as before. Certain of our players came home to find that their counties had turned against them as a matter of policy, and some relationships have still not been patched up to this day, but Essex took the realistic view that John and I had taken up employment while we were not under contract to the county and that what we had done was very unlikely to damage county cricket in any way. Doug Insole did come to my house to see me, and both John and I made an appointment to see our chairman, 'Tiny' Waterman, at his home in Epping. Neither man was exactly delighted by what we had done but there was no animosity – we agreed to disagree in each instance. Doug quoted the Gleneagles agreement to lend weight to the case against our tour but my argument was that the team was neither 'international' nor 'representative' so the agreement was irrelevant. We both came to the conclusion that Gleneagles can be interpreted in a number of different ways and, as such, is an unsatisfactory agreement.

Essex were not slow to appreciate that they were likely to be the winners from the situation, in that John and I would be available all the time, barring injury, for three summers in which we might otherwise have both been frequently taken away from the county side to play for England. Partly due to this, the county stood to be more successful on the field, and consequently more prosperous off it. This was not, unhappily, the view of everyone in the game, and towards the fag-end of the summer of 1982 we were all obliged to accept that any attempt to have our suspensions reduced or overruled in court was likely to end in failure.

The decision was not taken lightly. Linklaters and Paines had been thorough in compiling their dossier on the case, questioning all the players who went about their reasons for accepting, taking statements from members of the Test and County Cricket Board and closely scrutinising our county contracts. They then took an opinion from Robert Alexander QC, who officiated at the Packer case.

Ideally, of course, we would have liked to win our appeal against sentence without litigation and, although this was quite possibly a fanciful hope, we were invited to send representatives along to discuss the matter with the Test and County Cricket Board. This was progress. I even liked to think it might provide the breakthrough we all wanted. But it was a blind alley.

The meeting, the last of what seemed an endless series of formal and informal gatherings since the seeds of the tour were first sown, took place on Monday, 26 July at the city offices of the TCCB's appointed solicitors, Slaughter and May. There was reason to think that progress had been made, as we were asked to send along a selection of players whose careers had been at different stages when the ban was implemented. We chose Emburey and myself, as current England players, Boycott and Amiss as old players whose Test days may well have been over, and Les Taylor as an example of one who had not yet played for England.

The timing of the meeting created difficulties as we were all engaged in championship matches, but the board gave special dispensation allowing us to absent ourselves for however long the discussions took. Essex were playing Leicestershire at Grace Road and the game was interestingly poised when Les Taylor and myself left the ground on Monday afternoon to drive to London, both wondering just what was in store for us next.

We had been sentenced in our absence, without an opportunity to plead our defence, which under the laws of natural justice is surely wrong. Perhaps the board felt, or were advised, that they were morally bound to give us that chance, but they gave us no cause to believe there was any possibility they might relent. The players and their solicitors sat on one side of a long table, the board officials and their own legal men on the other, and I rapidly formed the impression that in terms of securing any change of heart we were wasting our time being there. Our case was put, lucidly by the solicitors and honestly by the players, and the men from Lord's were not entirely unsympathetic. But the crucial point was made when we were told the board were satisfied that our presence in the England team would lead to cancellation of tours by India, Pakistan and West Indies. It then became clear that, since their costly defeat in the High Court by Kerry Packer, the TCCB had adjusted their constitution so that they were, in effect, an employers' association. This, apparently, offered them protection from the 'restraint of trade' law that we had been hoping to pursue because they had only to prove they were acting in the interests of the majority of their members (i.e. the counties and their players) to legally justify bans or exclusions on a minority.)

In their case, the justification was plain. If the tours by India and Pakistan that summer had been abandoned, the loss of income would have been severe. Many counties rely, probably overmuch, on their annual payout from Test match receipts and could have been plunged into serious financial trouble. The contest was over almost before it had begun. No one had cause to get angry or unpleasant, indeed the whole meeting was conducted in such a cordial atmosphere that both sides enjoyed a drink together afterwards. But, as far as we were concerned, this was the end of our hopes of remission.

Our threat had been that we would take the matter to court and, although the thought did not appeal to any of us, we would have carried it through. It would not even have cost the players a penny of their own money as an anonymous benefactor had come forward to guarantee meeting all the costs – even I do not know who he is. His money, however, was never needed as our advice was that it was far from certain we would win. The board had taken new advice since the Packer days and there was no doubting their confidence in their position nor, legally at least, the fact that they were on pretty solid ground.

It might be worth saying here that we had reached this stage quite unaided by any other cricketing body. If something similar had happened to workers in any of Britain's trade unions, action would have been concerted – for better or for worse. But the cricketers' 'trade union' has never been a militant body and there was no move from them to support us in any way. We had tried to put our case at the annual meeting of the 'union' – properly known as The Cricketers' Association – just before the season began. We felt it was important to put our point of view and to gauge the feelings of the average county professionals. I expected some aggressive opposition and I was not disappointed. In my own speech, I repeated what I had been saying all along, which is that more than 50 English cricketers earn a living in South Africa each winter and I did not feel that we should be treated differently just because we had clubbed together to play some highly-publicised and competitive matches there. The view against us was probably put most accurately by Alastair Hignell, then of Gloucestershire, who said that when he first heard of the tour he had been envious and interested but that, when he discovered it was a potential threat to his livelihood, he had turned very much against it.

Various other players spoke, both for and against, and then some rather confusing voting took place in which two motions – one of which appeared to be supporting us and the other condemning us – were both carried. A further motion, quite plainly against us, was then put to the meeting and carried, however, and it was at this point that Geoff Boycott interposed disastrously.

He had waited until towards the end of the meeting to say anything at all but when he did speak he clearly meant to leave a lasting impression. He told the meeting that if we received no support from our fellow members we would have no option but to fight the case in court. What he was saying to his county colleagues, at least to their way of thinking, was 'to hell with you – we will take you all on whatever the consequences.' It was an ultimatum. And it did not go down well.

Whatever sympathy we had gained during the course of the meeting vanished in a matter of seconds. Nobody likes being threatened, especially where the matter of money, status and possibly envy is involved, and for Boycott to address his fellow players in that manner was red rag to a bull. Several jumped up now to speak passionately and aggressively about greed and selfishness and the original thread of rational thinking became lost forever. Until then, my over-riding feeling had been that a lot of players were theoretically all in favour of the kind of tour we had undertaken and would love to have had the opportunity themselves. But, because they had been told that their jobs might be at risk, they voted against their principles. From our point of view it was a shame, but no one could be blamed for seeing it that way.

One point raised at the meeting, however, had my complete support – the more so because it was voiced by a man who had more to gain than most by the exclusion of 15 players from the international scene. Robin Jackman had flirted only briefly and very controversially with Test cricket, joining the tour of West Indies in 1981 as a replacement for Bob Willis and almost immediately being deported from Guyana because he had spent time in South Africa. Now, however, with bowlers such as Old, Lever, Hendrick and Taylor out of the way, he could look forward to the prospect of more Test caps which, indeed, he was to win later that season. But when Robin rose in the Edgbaston banqueting suite, which is the traditional setting for the association's meetings, he said he could not believe the logic of banning 15 English players for one short visit to South Africa if, as seemed almost certain, a South African called Allan Lamb was about to make his England debut against India.

There have been, as I have constantly said, anomalies all down the line in this country's dealings with South Africa, both on the sports field and in business. One such was the honour bestowed on the deservedly popular England rugby captain Billy Beaumont in 1982 when, two years earlier, he had led the British Lions on an official tour to South Africa which drew angry political reactions. But I cannot believe there has ever been anything quite as ironical as Allan Lamb's selection for England.

On a personal level I have nothing against Allan at all. He is a very fine batsman who, quite justifiably, decided to make use of the laws to qualify to play for England after spending all his formative years in South Africa. He was about to become eligible for the first time when we toured South Africa and he knew that to join up with the team of his birth and play against us would render his qualification period a complete waste of time – he would never have been considered for England. So, despite repeated requests, he refused to play against us, either for Western Province or for the South African XI.

Sure enough, on 2 June that year, Lamb made his England debut in the first Prudential Trophy one-day international against India, and he has held his place since. Also in 1982, Ian Greig – brother of Tony – made his debut for England, as did Chris Smith in 1983, both having qualified through having British parents and British citizenship.

To the best of my knowledge, the non-white Test-playing countries have never raised a murmur of complaint about the presence of any of these men in an England side. So they are content to play against people who were born and brought up in South Africa, but refuse to play against people who make a single visit. Is there any sensible reasoning behind that?

6

The man who said no to £45,000

I felt sick at heart the day Keith Fletcher was sacked as England captain. Sick for him, because I knew how much the job meant to him, and sick at the situation which must have brought it all to such a shocking end. No matter what explanations had been produced for the decision – and to my certain knowledge, none were ever given to Keith – I could never have accepted it as being just. But then, perhaps I knew more of the salient circumstances than the men who ditched him.

I had been with 'Fletch' all the way through India and Sri Lanka where, presumably, his leadership was felt to have been inadequate in some way. I had helped keep any hint of the South African tour plans from him so that he would not feel his loyalties being compromised. And then I had personally telephoned him to make the offer of a small fortune to drop everything and join us in Johannesburg. He turned me down, and I never had any doubts why.

Every cricketer dreams at some age of captaining England. To the huge majority, the thought never develops beyond being an idle, passing fantasy, never to be fulfilled. But to the lucky few, it grows into a genuine possibility. With 'Fletch' it had been different. He had done his time with England, as a batsman in the front-line for almost a decade. In and out of the side with a frequency which either suggests unusual riches of talent or muddled selectorial thinking, he had overcome hazards like the hatred of the Yorkshire crowd (still visible and now mutual) and the mental ordeal of facing Lillee and Thomson at their most ferocious, and still emerged with an admirable Test match average of nearly 40 after more than fifty caps. The cynical – and there have been many who seem to find 'the Gnome' an easy target for sarcasm – remember only the undignified sight of his toiling against extreme pace and bounce in Australia, and write him off as someone not good enough when the heat was on. They forget both his consistency before and after that tour and the fact that he was by no means the worst affected batsman.

When he bowed out of the England side after the 1977 Melbourne Centenary Test, Fletcher was approaching 33 and it was commonly agreed he would not be back. But still he went on making his annual mountain of runs at county level and astutely captaining an Essex side which had, partly through his ministrations, become one of England's most successful sides. So when Ian Botham found the England skipper's job all too much, and Mike Brearley made it plain he would not tour again, it suddenly began to occur to people within the game that they could do worse than revive Keith's England career, bring him back as part of the management rather than the shop-floor.

'Fletch' had long since given up. The dream had died, and he had come to terms with it, thankful for the caps he had won and content to play out his career in the county environment he still enjoyed so much. But if the offer ever came, he was certainly not about to turn it down. The phone call was duly made on a Sunday morning in August 1981. Alec Bedser, then still chairman of England's selectors, rang the Fletcher household in a dreamy little village near Dunmow and 'invited' Keith to lead the touring team to India. I don't suppose he had to wait long for his answer.

I well remember the genuine excitement and pleasure within our dressing-room. We were in the midst of Colchester week, a huge crowd had gathered for the John Player League match and 'Fletch', so typically, was more concerned that we should not be distracted from winning than with the attention being feasted upon him. He said he wanted it to be a totally normal day and that if there was any celebrating to be done, it should wait until we also had a victory to enjoy in our quest for the John Player League title.

We did, however, manage to embarrass him in characteristic Essex fashion. As we took the field, our secretary Peter Edwards announced over the public address system, to all who did not know it already, that 'Fletch' was now captain of country as well as county. In his own inimitable way, 'Fletch' shuffled onto the field with his head sunk low into his chest, blissfully unaware that the rest of us, orchestrated by the inevitable Ray East, had halted at the pavilion gate. Keith was half-way to the middle, loudly cheered by the crowd, before he realized he was on a solo voyage.

He took it in good part, of course. Everyone has to learn that, at Essex, practical jokes are part of the curriculum, but 'Fletch', in his amusingly dry way, is just as often the promoter of a joke or a prank, when the time is right. There are many, many stories about him, usually relating to things he has said and often making much of his inability to sound his r's, but one of the best – aptly summarising the irony of the man – is told by Tony Lewis.

Tony was captain of the England tour of India and Pakistan in 1972–73 – a tour which ran into crowd unrest on more than one occasion. At Bombay, apparently, the team received a written threat from the PLO that they were planning to murder certain members of the team. Remembering the Munich massacre no one took this to be a joke, and for some time the Test to be played there was in real jeopardy. Eventually, after making certain stipulations regarding the tightening of security arrangements, including the positioning of police on all roof-tops in the immediate vicinity, England nervously agreed that the game could go on – that, in Lewis's view, to call it off would have been a general invitation for terrorists to disrupt sport around the world. Obviously, however, there was a good deal of apprehension in the camp when England took the field and 'Fletch', although stationed at first slip, insisted on walking into the position before each delivery so that he was not a sitting target. When his captain questioned him on this tactic, he replied: 'It's all right for you, skip. They'll shoot you in the leg so that they can get you lbw again.'

If the questionable quality of Indian umpiring was on his mind then, it was certainly very prominent when he returned nine years later as captain. On this occasion, the series was won and lost in Bombay, despite it being only the First Test, and, although England played so badly as to deserve nothing more than defeat, the efforts of umpire K. B. Ramaswamy were not appreciated by many of the Englishmen present. As the series wore on, the umpiring developed into a complex with us, culminating in 'Fletch', of all people, knocking off a bail with his bat in sheer frustration at being given out in dubious circumstances at Bangalore.

Nobody has ever stated that this was the primary reason for him losing the captaincy but, with Peter May taking over from Alec Bedser and immediately making firm pronouncements on the subject of on-field discipline, it would be a short-odds bet that it had plenty to do with the decision. Now, I am perfectly certain that Keith has regretted his impulsive action from that day to this, and he issued a rapid public apology for it at the time. He would accept that it was not the kind of behaviour English cricket likes to associate with its captains and, moreover, that it was a poor reflection on him at a time when he was urging us all to put the umpiring out of our minds and exercise complete self-control.

Having said all that, it was surely not enough evidence upon which to dispatch him to the wilderness. For one thing, none of the selectors responsible for the change had been in India, so they were relying entirely on the manager's report and the British newspapers. For another, Peter May himself had never been to India, and until you have toured there it is quite impossible to appreciate the peculiarly maddening pressures which mount in the existence of a touring cricketer.

My main assertion, however, is that there were bigger issues to be considered than one brief abberation on a bad day in Bangalore. English cricket had undergone an upheaval since our departure for South Africa and – although it could justifiably be said I am not speaking from a position of strength – I would have thought it was the right time to reward loyalty. Leaving aside now the justification of the ban imposed on myself and the other players who toured, I think it fair to say we would all have expected to be sacked from the England captaincy if we had held the job at the time of going to South Africa, in the same way as Tony Greig had plainly resigned himself to losing the position when he organized the recruitment of English players for Kerry Packer. Greig had betrayed a certain trust placed in him when he accepted the captaincy, which made the post untenable, but the courts decided there were no grounds for suspending him as a player.

Fletcher had steadfastly sustained his allegiance to English cricket and to the Test and County Cricket Board. It is not easy to turn down £45,000 when for most of your 20-year career you have been earning a fraction of that for each year's work, but 'Fletch' turned his back on it. His name was clear. There were no charges to answer. And that was how he wanted it to be, because he had achieved only half of his ambitions. He had still not led England in a home Test, and I think that meant more to him than anything in the world at that time. Nobody, in this life, should expect anything as a matter of right, but K. W. R. Fletcher had every reason to suppose he would not be disappointed in his aims. He had, it is true, been in charge of a losing team overseas, but that was nothing new (in fact it has recently become a habit). He had, in the view of the England players, done a good job under conditions made slightly more difficult by the fact that he was returning to the side after a long absence to captain a number of well-established players. Despite that, he took and kept command, achieved the respect of everyone and made his usual quota of runs without showing the tendency of some to be weighed down by the responsibilities. No captain, I suggest, could have come away from that Indian tour with the result any different, and many might have coped less manfully than 'Fletch' with the problems.

His attitude towards those of us who went to South Africa was enlightening. Neither he nor anyone else in the Essex dressing-room caused any problems for John and I – there was no animosity or overt jealousy. Keith Pont, who had been in Cape Town at the time, delighted in telling everyone how he used to turn up in The Oaks section of the ground for our games brandishing a giant banner saying 'I'm Available'. I had the impression that most of the staff would have thought, if not actually done, the same. 'Fletch' understood why we had accepted the offer and never tried to tell us we should not have done. He is all for players earning what they can while they are in the game and often makes the point that a cricketer's active life is a short one and there are no guarantees for retirement. He did not, however, believe that there should have been any moaning about the severity of the punishment we received. He was quoted somewhere as having said: 'They got what they deserved'. I am not certain that is an accurate summary of his feelings, but he did believe that everyone should have gone in with their eyes open, alert to all the possible consequences . . . exactly as he was when he rejected the offer. Much later, when the axe had fallen on him, he made no secret of the fact that he would not say 'no' again.

Keith was the original two-time loser. He turned down a fortune to save a job he loved. Then lost the job. In my view, although he received no ban from Tests as we did, he lost more than anyone from the episode because in subsequent years, although widely accepted as the best leader in the county game – not to mention still being one of the best batsmen, 'Fletch' has not so much as been mentioned in connection with England selection. He is, it seems, banished for ever, a harsh way to treat a man who has served the game so well.

It had looked for all the world as if his reappointment was a mere formality when he was asked to lead MCC against the champion county, Notts, in the first of the 1982 season's showpiece matches at Lord's. But then came a surprise. The traditional match between MCC and the tourists, in this instance our recent friends from India, was scheduled for the third week of May and the MCC team was, unusually, to be chosen by the England selectors. The side they picked was not especially surprising, except that Fletcher was not included and David Gower was nominated as captain. This naturally began some furious speculation in the national papers that Gower was being lined up to take over the England job. To me, this seemed an absurd idea as David had not even graduated to captaining his county, Leicestershire. I did not believe that the England selectors could seriously be contemplating giving the number one job to one so woefully underprepared for it. What is more, I told 'Fletch' so, and, although I think the snub had caused him some concern, he still at this stage felt that he was likely to keep the job.

It was made known that the captaincy issue was to be resolved during the MCC match and an announcement made on the final afternoon. It came around four o'clock. I was at home, Essex not having a game, and I happen to know Fletch was in his garden. I was astonished. I can only hazard an informed guess as to how he felt. The captain was not to be Fletcher. Nor Gower. Instead it was to be Bob Willis.

Now, I happen to like Bob very much, quite apart from admiring him enormously as a fast bowler and as a thinker on the game. But there is a vast difference between being number two, a task he had performed with credit for some years, and being out at the front of the troops. I wondered if he had the personality for the job. I also thought it an unsuitable marriage with the stresses and remoteness of fast bowling. But most of all, on that Friday afternoon in May, I wondered why on earth the change had been made at all.

'Fletch' has since related his own numbed reactions to the brief phone call he received from Peter May. He went off alone, driving he knew not where, just wanting to be alone with his sorrow. He later said he parked his car somewhere way out in the country and sat in it for a long while, trying to work out why it had happened. Peter May had not told him, and he could not come up with a good enough reason himself.

The following morning was an ordeal for him, an embarrassment for the rest of the Essex players. I think we all felt like interlopers at a family funeral, as if we were intruding on his private grief. I cannot think of any other occasion when the Essex dressing-room has been as quiet as it was that morning, when no one knew what to say. When one of the side is dropped by England, as has happened on various occasions during my career, the player concerned is consoled by a few muttered 'bad luck's, the ice is broken by a joke or two and the matter is then forgotten. But this was different. 'Bad luck' would have been a hopelessly inadequate comment and I don't think anyone ventured it. Instead, there was virtual silence as we changed for our Benson and Hedges Cup qualifier against Hampshire at Chelmsford.

Someone, I can't recall exactly which of our comedians, tried to make Keith laugh by telling him he should have taken the £45,000. But as jokes go, it sank without trace, and we went out into the field led by a captain who was not quite with us. 'Fletch' was mentally miles away, distracted and visibly disturbed by something it had apparently been quite beyond his control to influence. He did not talk about it, so nobody else did, either, but throughout that weekend he was very far from being the forceful skipper we all knew so well. It seemed utterly appropriate when, chasing a modest

Hampshire score of 130, we crashed to a hideous 14 for six, Fletcher being one of the cheap dismissals for Malcolm Marshall and Kevin Emery. But Stuart Turner and David East concocted victory from this mess and probably saved 'Fletch' from going home in even more suicidal mood.

He recovered his composure and his grip on the team during the following week. He also recovered his form with a vengeance and, whether or not it was through an aching desire to prove that he was still good enough to bat for England, he made two masterful centuries in successive matches, while privately, I suspect, coming to the conclusion that if England did ask him to play in a Test match as batsman alone, he would politely decline. I can't say I blamed him, either. In the aftermath of the shock, we at Essex had plenty of opportunity to weigh up our debts to 'Fletch' and to assess exactly what influence he had wielded in making us the team we were, the individuals we were.

He has been captain throughout my time on the Essex staff, although I played a game or two in 1973 under his predecessor, Brian 'Tonker' Taylor. When Keith took on the job, he had already been in county cricket 12 years and been playing for England over a period of six years. By today's standards he was vastly experienced, and lacked for nothing in grounding, but more important is the fact that he had not wasted his apprenticeship. His knowledge of cricket and cricketers is wide, his mind remarkably retentive. He will assess the strengths and weaknesses of batsmen very accurately, and thereafter never forget them and how to counter them. He will set fields from memory and invariably he will be right. Not very many captains I have known can claim to have possessed that gift.

Keith has a likeable, easy-going personality but he obtains the respect of his players through his own performance and professionalism. He likes the lads to enjoy themselves; it has always been an Essex trait to play hard off the field as well as on it and I hope it always will be. But, whereas in quite recent times I have the impression Essex played the game primarily for fun, now we expect and are expected to win, and 'Fletch' has occasionally demonstrated how he will stamp very firmly on anyone straying out of line.

During my time in the game, there have been only two outstanding English captains, Fletcher being one and Mike Brearley the other. Whereas Brearley was given the time to achieve his marvels with the England team, Keith was not, and I honestly do not believe there is much to separate them as leaders. There are, however, some interesting comparisons to make.

England captains should, by definition, have the best players in their side. So, accepting that the ability is present, it is their job to mould the individuals into a unit and to make them want to play together. It is unarguably true that players try harder for some captains than for others, but I have never met anyone who did not give 100 per cent for either Brearley or Fletcher. 'Brears' is tighter on off-field discipline, not entirely subscribing to the Fletcher view that professionals should know how to take care of themselves. Keith believes players should basically spend their free time exactly how they please so long as they are fully fit and alert to resume their game the following morning. Mike, while by no means being a bully for curfews and temperance, takes a slightly tougher line.

As motivators, they are very different. Mike is highly intelligent and extremely lucid. Because of this, he comes over very well in giving team-talks, not only purveying sound good sense but putting it across to his team in a most articulate manner. Keith is seldom lost for a word, but he does his motivating briefly and simply.

'Fletch', in fact, is not keen on team meetings and I cannot recall a single occasion when he has called us together to discuss an individual Essex match. When he led England, however, some meetings were clearly essential and I well remember the occasion when he called the bowlers together before the Second Test in Bangalore. We were already one down and Keith wanted to sort out fields and tactics against each of the Indian batsmen as we tried to manoeuvre the equalising win. The trouble was, every time a batsman's name was mentioned, Ian Botham would take over:

'Don't worry about him, I'll bounce him out.'

'He can't play the short ball.'

'He's scared of my bouncer, I'll take care of him.'

And so we went on through the team, the rest of us convulsed with laughter as Ian won the Test single-handed with the short-pitched bowling of which he is so fond. History relates that India only batted once at Bangalore, scoring 428 with Ian taking two for 137 . . . but his confidence is not something we ever discouraged.

Keith probably needed little help in this direction anyway, as his field-placing is at least a match for Brearley's. If one has to find a fault with the Fletcher style of captaincy it would be that he is not the most diplomatic of men. He can sometimes seem abrupt, almost rude, to officials and outsiders who are interfering with his routine, and he is not the most adept at handing out the consoling platitudes when someone is left out of the side. He gives tremendous encouragement to his bowlers, in the field, and to batsmen before they go in, but when things have gone wrong and a word in the ear might make all the difference, I don't think it occurs to Keith that he might have a contribution to make.

It is, however, very harsh to pick holes in the part he has played at Essex over the years. For ten seasons he had a settled side and everyone said that we would be on the slide as soon as the team began to break up. But Keith was always a step ahead, combining with the club's coaches to bring in the young, new blood at exactly the right time and ensure that success would be perpetuated.

I feel certain he could have done as good a job for England as he has for Essex. I believe he would have had a stabilising effect on the Test team through a very trying period, and I am convinced he should still be in charge now. But, for whatever reason, it was not to be.

7

Out of sight, out of form

Only once in my life have I ever asked to be dropped. It happened midway through the first summer of my suspension, when I was mentally and physically at my lowest ebb, but I was firmly talked out of it all by Keith Fletcher. Not even my Essex team-mates knew that I wanted to be left out. I never told them, and I am pretty sure 'Fletch' didn't. I am grateful to him both for that, and for his faith in me, because it was not long afterwards that the tide turned and the runs began to flow.

Every player goes through a bad patch now and again. Even Vivian Richards, commonly acknowledged as the greatest in the world, suffered a sequence of low scores in Tests during 1984 in England and Australia. If he has to endure it, there is hope for the most modest of club cricketers as he unbuckles his pads after a third successive nought. The major problem lies in diagnosing the reason for failure and then locating the cure.

In my case, it did not take a vivid imagination to conclude that my problem was a variation on a hangover. Nothing to do with alcohol, everything to do with a mind confused by the banishment from Test cricket, the lingering possibility of a court case and a misguided resolution to live up to what it seemed were everyone's expectations of a bonanza first full season back in county cricket.

Everyone I met, on my return from South Africa, assured me with great confidence that I was certain to make 2,000 runs in championship cricket alone and show the England selectors exactly what they were missing. I could not agree. Although my form had been good and my confidence high both in India and South Africa, I had never made anything approaching 2,000 runs in a county season and, even allowing for the fact that I was likely to play almost every game, I could not envisage doing it now. I have no illusions about my own qualities – I can play big innings and I will get my share of hundreds each season, but I am not in the category of Geoff Boycott or Dennis Amiss, players who will churn out runs consistently, match after match, week after week. I tend to play in a fairly adventurous manner and, by its very nature, my style will lead to some early dismissals. I might win a few games, but I will also have a few bad trots.

In the early weeks of the 1982 season, however, it was not just an ordinary slump. I knew I was not my usual self. I felt disorientated by my situation, and it was getting through to my batting in a way I was not accustomed to. The fluency had gone, and with it went much of my confidence.

I would have understood it more easily if it could have been attributed to missing Test cricket. But I have to admit that hardly came into it at all. I expected to miss the England atmosphere much more than I actually did. This probably related to my boredom in India where, despite being fairly successful, I had mentally tired of the tour, but I still thought it odd that I could sit down to watch England playing on television during the summer of 1982 without experiencing a sensation of wishing I was there. I saw Geoff Cook and Chris Tavaré, two men who had turned down the chance of going to South Africa, open the batting in the First Test at Lord's and I wished them well. It gave me no sense of jealous pleasure when they both failed twice, and I could certainly never bring myself to hope that England would be beaten just because I was not being considered. Yet I knew I should be feeling some pangs of regret, some sense of loss. It worried me that it was not there.

Essex's season began disastrously, rallied to a certain extent and then tailed off again in the closing weeks. All in all, it was not a year to linger in the memory even if it did have some redeeming features. Within the first month of the season we had contrived to play so poorly that we were virtually out of contention for three of the four main competitions. We had been beaten in our first four John Player League games, we were out of the Benson and Hedges Cup at the group stage and we had lost narrowly to Middlesex and heavily to Sussex in the Schweppes County Championship. In this competition there was, of course, plenty of time left to put matters to rights but we were performing so inadequately that I would doubt if the most reckless gambler would have chanced a few pounds on us.

Surrey and Kent comfortably beat us in the opening zonal games of the Benson and Hedges Cup but, after somehow salvaging that lost cause against Hampshire on the day following Fletcher's removal from the England captaincy, there was some consolation for the team – and some relief for yours truly – in our final group game, against Sussex at Hove. We were put in by John Barclay, which must have haunted him for some time. I scored 198 not out and 'Fletch' 101 not out; together we put on an unbroken 268 for the third wicket and our 55-overs total was a mammoth 327 for two. I am told that my innings represented the highest score in a one-day match in England, and I have certainly seldom batted quite so dominantly. I ended a memorable personal game by taking three cheap wickets and we went home in good spirits with a win by 114 runs.

Euphoria was short-lived. Back in the Championship, I just could not put together a decent run of scores. People reached the natural conclusion that I was suffering from lack of motivation, that without the incentive of England caps I could not generate the necessary self-interest in cricket to maintain my standards. Perhaps they were right. Certainly, I was struggling to get properly motivated for every game, but then that is nothing new for me. Throughout my career, I feel I would have made many more runs if only I could retain concentration for long periods, content myself with crease-occupation and aim single-mindedly at the long innings.

For a while, I convinced myself that things would come right. Very often, if I have started a season in poor form it has taken me some time to get back into a rhythm, whereas a good start breeds the confidence to keep things running smoothly. But when mid-July arrived and I was still short of 500 first-class runs, I was beginning to despair. It came to a head during Southend week, our annual cricket festival by the sea, much enjoyed by the players of Essex and our visitors alike – usually. This year, I feared, was not going to be much fun. On the opening day of the festival, a Saturday, I went out to bat before a modest crowd, while up at Trent Bridge England were in the field against Pakistan in the first of their one-day internationals for the Prudential Trophy. I had not yet seen anything of what looked on paper to be quite an exciting Pakistan line-up, but I was able to spend most of the day watching them on TV. I was out to the very first delivery of our match against Derbyshire – caught behind off Steve Oldham, the former Yorkshire fast bowler – and, although every opener suffers this ultimately gruesome fate once in a while, it was the last straw for me.

For a fortnight before that match, I had been turning over the possibility of asking to be rested. It was not something I contemplated lightly and nor, I feel, should any player, but it had reached the stage where I was thoroughly depressed with my form and could not come up with any good reasons for failure. The nearest to a solution was that I might simply have been trying too hard – straining mentally to live up to an image, and so playing in an unnatural, forced manner. But whatever the truth of it, I was waking up each morning without once looking forward to batting, which was both unusual and dangerous for someone who by nature loves playing cricket.

On the last day of that match I had two conversations which put me in a better frame of mind. I had already been out for the second time in the game, caught for 31 after battling to occupy the crease for a long period, and I was in the club caravan before play resumed, having some treatment on a niggling strain from our physiotherapist, Ray Cole. It must have been pretty obvious to all the lads that I was brooding about my failings, and 'Fletch' walked across from the dressing-room to the caravan, where he knew we could have a private talk. He asked me what my problem was. I told him I felt jaded with cricket as a whole, and pretty low about my loss of form. I just didn't feel right when I was batting, I told him, and, as I was really not contributing much at all to the team's efforts, would it not be a sensible idea to leave me out for a while and give one of our fringe players a chance to establish himself.

I am not sure what I expected Keith to say – maybe a gesture of support and then acquiescence to my suggestion. In my own mind, I certainly believed I would not be playing in our next match and had probably begun to think about the best way of refreshing myself away from the game for a while. But 'Fletch' swiftly disillusioned me. He turned down the idea point-blank, told me that I was a good player in whom he had great confidence and that no one was fretting or moaning about my form except myself. If I just kept going and played my natural game, he said, everything would soon come right. In other words, forget the idea of being dropped and get on with it.

Fletch wandered off and left me to ponder on the fact that it was the first time we had ever needed to have such a talk. Essex have never dropped me since I first established myself in the side; they are a county who remain traditionally loyal to their players through thick and thin and, although now we have a large enough squad for places to be precious and competition fierce, nobody is left out just on the basis of one or two failures.

I appreciated the vote of confidence from the skipper. Appreciated it, too, later in the day when Derbyshire's captain Barry Wood had a word with me. Barry has caused plenty of controversy in his time and might not be the most popular figure in one or two counties, but no one ever doubted his wholesale commitment to cricket and his knowledge of the game. He was going through a lean time himself but he pointed out to me his very simple philosophy. 'When you're struggling,' he said, 'just force yourself to remember there are always plenty of people worse off than you. We are paid for playing a game we enjoy – we should never sulk about it.'

It was good advice. I was pleased now to have been talked out of a rest and, if I was not exactly brimming with confidence again, I was at least seeing things in context, whereas before I had been blowing a relatively minor hiccough in my career into a major crisis.

Our next match was against Middlesex, starting at Southend the following day, and when Mike Brearley won the toss and put us in I ground out what may well rate among my least attractive, but was certainly among my most important and satisfying, innings. I made 60, followed it with an only slightly more positive 87 in the second innings, and, although I was still unable to relax as I would have liked, I fought it through on both occasions. *Wisden* recalls: 'Gooch, struggling for his true form, showed great determination in his two half-centuries.' That sums it up. It was the turning point of the season for me.

I scored another pair of fifties in our next match at Leicester – the game in which I went absent to talk legal language with the powers-that-be at Lord's – and then, after an irritating flop against Glamorgan, made the real breakthrough with 71 and 149 during a memorable contest with Kent at Canterbury. My second-innings hundred occupied only 95 minutes and I could feel the fluency seeping back into my game. In the closing fixtures of the season I scored another two centuries and finished up, remarkably, with 1,632 runs in first-class games alone. It was my best-ever figure and it made me Essex's highest run-scorer that year, statistics which mask the story.

The setbacks of that season taught me a few lessons, as much about myself as anything. I also rediscovered some facts of life about batting. When confidence is undermined, a player's entire game can be shot to pieces. The harder he tries to correct the faults, the worse the problems can become because his thinking gets to be muddled. He may try to go and blast his way out of trouble, playing attacking shots to balls he would never normally contemplate hitting; or he may go out intent on grafting until he eliminates virtually every attacking stroke and his supply of runs dries up completely. Eventually, having tried all the crazy options and not found one which works, he has no idea what he is doing at the crease at all. His only consolation, if he is a good enough player and he can see the wood for the trees, is that one day the breaks will go his way, and everything will change. Until that happens, however, it can be a painful experience.

Twelve months earlier, in July 1981, I had been through a similar period of soul-searching, but on this occasion the subject was not my form for Essex but for England. At county level I could have had no complaints, as I had already achieved something I believe to be unique in scoring a century in each of the four major competitions during the course of the season. But at England level I was unarguably in a slump which threatened my place. It had all seemed so unlikely when I came back from West Indies a few months earlier feeling at the very top of my form. I had scored 116 out of England's 224 at Bridgetown despite the sickening sorrow of my good friend Kenny Barrington's sudden death, and then 153 out of 285 at

Kingston where we were surrounded by more guns than I have ever seen used to protect a cricket team. In cricket, however, you really are only as good as your last innings, and the Ashes series against Australia that summer was a personal horror story. I made 10 and 6 in a four-wicket defeat at Trent Bridge, 44 and 20 in a draw at Lord's and then, worst of all, I was out twice in a day, for two and nought, at Headingley.

Headingley and 1981 need only be mentioned in the same breath to a cricket lover to conjure up unforgettable images of Ian Botham's dramatic 149 not out when we looked likely to be beaten by an innings, and Bob Willis's frenetic, inspired fast bowling which snatched perhaps the most improbable victory in the history of Test cricket. Mike Brearley, who had retaken the captaincy for that match, was instantly regarded as some mystical guru, Botham and Willis were promoted above Thatcher, Scargill, Paisley or whoever the political newsmakers of the week might have been and built up into supermen. My own failings suddenly assumed very little significance and while, after my dismissals, I had been darkly brooding on the likelihood of being left out and concluding that it would probably be the best thing that could happen, I now looked forward to the next game and felt relieved and grateful to be chosen.

I actually played in the next two Tests but scores of 21, 21, 10 and 5 were patently insufficient to warrant any further faith from the selectors and, having been part of three of the most fantastic victories any cricketer can ever have experienced, I took my leave, went back to county cricket and scored a stack of runs in the last few weeks of the Essex season, feeling in a far happier frame of mind than I would have done if the Botham-Willis miracle had never happened and I had been dropped after Headingley. Sometimes, circumstances and unconnected events can direct one's mood and fate to an extraordinary degree.

Essex's failure to challenge for any of the available honours in 1982 was a major disappointment to us all. In 1979 we had ended 103 years of waiting with the championship and the Benson and Hedges Cup. In 1980 we reached Lord's for the Benson and Hedges Cup final again, only to throw it away against Northants. In 1981 we ended a frustrating habit of finishing runners-up in the John

Player League by winning it for the first time. But in 1982, just as everyone at the club had begun to grow accustomed to success and, in many cases, to expect it, we achieved nothing.

Coming to terms with mediocrity after several buoyant years is in many ways more difficult than never winning anything at all. After all, our supporters had endured plenty of seasons of emptiness and accepted it without too much complaint. Even up to the time when I joined the club, Essex were considered a 'fun' side, who would usually be entertaining to watch, played cricket in the right manner and scraped by financially thanks to some frightening economies. But they were never expected to actually win anything. The attitude amongst the players in those days was also markedly different from what it is today, and the greatest changes have been in the fielding. There was no diving and precious little sprinting done by the Essex players of old; if you could not pick the ball up as it passed, or maybe stop it with a boot, you escorted it to the boundary at a gentle pace. Essex were not unique in this very amateurish approach, but the older players tell me they were among the worst. Despite having some distinguished cricketers in the ranks over the years, honours seemed to be something which a few of the other counties carved up amongst themselves. Essex were not among the runners.

Once the euphoria of 1979 hit the county, however, everything changed. Our headquarters at Chelmsford, until quite recently a pleasant but sparsely appointed riverside ground, has dramatically expanded to a point where it would be barely recognizable to anyone returning there after an absence of a few years. Its facilities are now superb and it could realistically hope to stage an international match (as it did during the 1983 World Cup) without complete chaos resulting. Our support, always loyal but often thin on the ground, has swelled enormously, and the one-day matches on our home grounds, in particular, now draw very healthy crowds indeed. Most important of all, of course, the attitude of the players has been sharpened by success. We are now very much a professional sporting unit and, while that does not mean we have ceased enjoying ourselves – if that ever happened, I think we would also stop winning – we approach each game with a commitment and will to succeed which, with all due respect, was probably not matched by some of our predecessors.

With the whole operation, then, geared up for further advancement, it came hard to everyone to have to accept a return to the ranks of the also-rans. By some standards, finishing seventh in the Championship and fifth in the John Player League might be thought a perfectly agreeable effort. By Essex's recent standards it was cause for a winter-long inquest on our behalf, and much muttering around the shires that the bubble had burst and we would now no longer be a threat to the more established big guns.

I have already recorded that our season had crashed off the rails in the opening weeks. It is virtually impossible to recover from losing the opening four Sunday games and still challenge for honours in that competition, for instance. Yet so dramatic was the turnaround in our fortunes that we threatened for a while to achieve the impossible.

Our four defeats occupied May and we were bottom of the table, inexplicable for the reigning champions and a side who liked to think they had to a large degree mastered the tactics of the 40-overs game. Then on 6 June, it rained. Chelmsford was flooded and, when we arrived at the usual hour of 12 noon for our pre-match lunch, it seemed a mere formality to abandon our game against Somerset, gratefully accept the two points on offer to each side for a no-result, and go home. Our administrative staff were much too resourceful to meekly accept a lost Sunday, however, and they had summoned the local fire brigade in an effort to pump the lying water off the ground. Our army of Sunday supporters helped out and, to the amazement of us all, umpires David Constant and Sam Cook were able to declare conditions fit for the minimum ten-overs-a-side contest. The enterprise of everyone who helped dry out the ground that afternoon turned the tide for us in more than just the literal sense. Wc won that match by onc run, our followers being treated to an absolute thriller for their efforts, and went on to win seven more Sunday games in succession, most of them by wide margins.

By 8 August, when we annihilated Kent by ten wickets and I managed to smash a car windscreen in hitting one of my three sixes at Canterbury, we had somehow moved into clear third place in the table, only Sussex and Middlesex still above us. We knew, however, that to have any real chance of catching the leaders we had to win our final four games as well, and that proved beyond us. We lost by five runs to Gloucestershire at Cheltenham and then, in one of the most spectacular Sunday games I have played in, found ourselves overhauled by Warwickshire after scoring 299 for four batting first. In the event it made no difference – Sussex just kept on winning, and deservedly took the trophy by a clear 12 points – but although we finished just out of the prize money we had at least reasured ourselves that we had not lost the knack of playing the short game.

Our failures in the other limited-overs competitions were probably more depressing. Elimination at the group stage of the Benson and Hedges Cup, following two successive appearances in the final in 1979 and 1980, was a major blow, but we began the knockout tournament, the NatWest Bank Trophy, with high hopes of improving upon our best previous effort as beaten semi-finalists. Having received a bye in the first round, we were drawn at home to neighbours Kent in the second. The club was delighted, as this guaranteed a big crowd and substantial revenue; it was, however, a challengingly difficult game for us. 'Fletch' guided us through it with a superbly paced innings of 97 in our total of 269, which proved way beyond Kent's compass and swept us into a quarter-final confrontation with the county which has probably become our fiercest rivals over the years, for a number of reasons – Yorkshire.

The reasons for Keith Fletcher's feelings towards Yorkshire, and in particular their so-called supporters, are well documented, but in recent years we have contested a number of tight, tense games with them in which an element of needle has crept in. Nothing much, just enough to make things that bit more interesting when we meet. This time we had to go to Headingley, which was a disadvantage anyway. Much more of a setback was the fact that 'Fletch' lost the toss and we were inevitably put into bat, because this was the year in which later rounds of the competition began at ten o'clock. It was a disastrous experiment as, far too often, the toss was utterly decisive. With mist still hanging over many grounds, and dew still on the surface, bowling conditions could hardly have been better. To be fair, we did not bat well, but the game was over as a contest well before lunch, when we stood at a miserable 51 for nine.

Stuart Turner, one of the most wholehearted triers in the game, refused to concede defeat, however, and with the support of Ray East he put on 81 for the last wicket, a record for 60-overs cricket. We were still woefully short of a challenging total, and Yorkshire cruised to victory by nine wickets, but at least some pride had been salvaged. Not surprisingly, 'Fletch' lodged a protest with Lord's over the ten o'clock starts, and he was not the only captain to pass on the feeling that it was making a mockery of the game. Significantly, the experiment was abandoned the following season. By then, however, it had already cost us any chance of 1982 honours.

The last six weeks of the season were academic as far as trophies were concerned and our championship form reflected the fact. After beating Glamorgan by seven wickets on 3 August, we failed to win one of our last eight matches, something which tempered my own satisfaction at regaining form.

If 1982 was a very easy year for most of us to file and forget, two Essex players at least will look back on it with considerable pleasure. Two starkly contrasting characters. Norbert Phillip, the West Indian allrounder who joined us in 1978 to replace Keith Boyce, scored almost 800 runs, took 82 wickets and confirmed once and for all that he had been a wise investment. And Derek Pringle, who had first played for us at the age of 19 before going off for four years at Cambridge University, finally joined us full-time – and found himself in the England team.

'Pring' had achieved very little in county cricket when he was selected for all three Tests against India, and one in the series which followed against Pakistan. His dramatic elevation was based almost entirely on his considerable success for Cambridge University and, while there is no denying that he made runs and took wickets against county sides, I think it is nowadays a false premise on which to select anyone for a Test team. Counties tend to view matches against the universities as an extra net practice in pleasant surroundings; no one likes to be beaten or to fail, but in truth the varsities have not been strong for years past and many counties field a number of second-team players and trialists against them. This is no environment in which to assess someone's ability to stand up to the rigours of Tests, and I fear Peter May (himself a former Cambridge student, but in the days when their cricket was formidably strong) and his fellow selectors were premature in selecting Derek, and possibly to his own detriment. Certainly, there were those in the Essex dressing-room who took a poor view of it. They had nothing against Derek personally – far from it, as his eccentric personality was an engaging addition to the team repertoire – but there were players in our side whose achievements over many seasons of county cricket completely dwarfed the Pringle record at that time. They simply considered him as a promising player; not, by any stretch of the imagination, an England allrounder.

I think in hindsight Derek would agree. He has become a very much better cricketer over the past two seasons, correcting a run-up problem through which he had threatened to give away games through no-balls and developing his game to a point where I would consider him among the best seam bowlers in England, quite apart from being a useful, clean hitter of the ball who can adapt to going in anywhere in the order. He should still have a future as a Test player – but in 1982 he was not ready.

He is still every bit the university eccentric. He wears leather ties, check shirts and wide black trousers, quite incongruous with his team blazer, and he is the equal of Phil Edmonds in being the most argumentative of cricketers I have ever come across. 'Pring' loves a debate, no matter what the subject. I sometimes think that if you put him in a corner with a broom, he would argue with it.

The only sense in which Derek could be compared with 'Nobby' is that both are allrounders and neither are among the most agile fielders in our side. There the similarity ends. 'Nobby' is a quiet, withdrawn man from the island of Dominica, a character that, for a year or two, the extroverts in our squad found it very hard to work out. He drinks halves when the rest of us drink pints and manages to say very little even when the dressing-room is in one of its slapstick moods. He accepts the ribbings which come his way in good spirit but only really shows his emotions at times of high tension on the field. Once or twice he has broken down in tears at the end of a one-day game; on other occasions, he has turned games our way with exuberant hitting and bowling which has the happy knack of producing wickets despite its apparently ungainly, stuttering run-up and occasional waywardness.

Ever since I first met him, I have never known 'Nobby' order anything but soup and steak in a restaurant. One night, we were in Canterbury after a Benson and Hedges Cup Saturday match, and 'Nobby' said he was going to his room to watch the football. He ordered ice cream to his room and asked me if I would act as waiter. Slightly taken aback by the request, I nevertheless carried the bowl of ice cream along the corridor, walked in and found Nobby watching Liverpool – his favourite team – with the sound turned down, and Bob Marley's reggae music blasting in his ear from a cassette player. This, I think, was probably his idea of paradise.

For some years, Nobby could not drive. Ray East usually collected him on his way to Chelmsford, but on one occasion Ray was with the second-team and David Acfield was nominated to stand in as chauffeur. We were due to start play at 11, but by ten-thirty there was no sign of 'Nobby' or David. Ten minutes later, with the rest of us changed and swapping stories of the likely excuses, David strolled into the dressing-room and announced that he had been unable to find the Phillip residence and so had abandoned the job. This was greeted with hoots of derision, but there was nothing more to be done than wait for developments, and it was lunch-time before our West Indian allrounder arrived on the ground, courtesy of the train service.

Although he now drives himself, it has not entirely cured the problem. Last summer 'Nobby' arrived in a squad of 13 at Chelmsford to be told that he was instead to play for the Second XI at Hampstead. He left Chelmsford at 11 o'clock for the drive into London but, at two o'clock, Ray East phoned to say he had still not arrived. He eventually made it at four, about four hours behind schedule, swearing that he had been to West Hampstead, South Hampstead and North Hampstead cricket clubs en route.

Phillip and Pringle, eccentrics both, and, in their separate ways, the Essex stars of 1982.

8

South African summers

The day England's selectors named their party to tour Australia was the day I first felt I was missing Test cricket. As usual, the announcement of the squad was made just before the end of the season; I was at Chelmsford for our final three-day game, against Northants, and Allan Lamb was in the process of making a fast hundred when his name was read out among the 16 to go on the trip. Derek Pringle had made it too, and so had the Northants captain, Geoff Cook. Pleased as I was for these good friends, I admit that I suddenly felt left out of things.

If the tour had been destined for anywhere else, I don't suppose I would have given it another thought but, like the majority of cricketers, I consider the Australian trip to be on a different plane to all others. Brash and provocative though the people may be, the country is basically hospitable, the food and the climate suit me fine and, most important of all, I enjoy playing cricket there. On the second of my two previous England tours Down Under I had been fairly successful and I would have looked forward to resuming battle with Rodney Hogg, Dennis Lillee and the rest.

The fact had to be faced. I would like to have gone, and I was sure to miss it. But I was not exactly consigned to a winter of tedium myself, and there was very little time in which to become maudlin about my situation. By the end of September, Brenda and I were on a flight to Cape Town, and it was very much like starting a new life.

Of all the places I have visited, both in the course of cricket trips and holidays, there are only two which make me think I could ever contemplate living outside England. Sydney is one, Cape Town the other.

My affections for thc marvellous city on the tip of South Africa's Cape Province date back to the winter of 1975–76. I had made my

Test debut the previous summer – a fraught experience involving a pair at Edgbaston and something not much better at Lord's against Ian Chappell's Australians – and my form had suffered badly when I returned to Essex after the experience. The winter put me straight. I played for the Green Point club in Cape Town, enjoyed the sunshine, drank the splendid red wine for which that province is famous, and generally wound down. Brenda and I made a lot of friends and we were happy to be going back there now, even if the circumstances were rather different.

Cape Town's attractions are not unlike those of Sydney. The beaches are spectacularly good, the scenery breathtaking, the climate perfect. Add to that the mountain ranges rising up behind the town, the facilities which match those of a holiday resort with a commercial centre, and it is not difficult to appreciate why so many people enjoy the place.

One thing spoiled my anticipation of the winter ahead. Western Province had never before engaged an overseas player. Now, following the South African Cricket Union's initiative in altering the registration rules to provide openings for myself and the other banned Englishmen, they were to have two. I was well aware that such a radical change would have caused great consternation, and no little resentment, if it had been implemented in England, and, as John Emburey and I flew out of Heathrow with our wives, we were both apprehensive about the reaction of the WP players. No doubt we were keeping South Africans out of their side; it was a new situation to us, used to being the native players in English cricket. The boot was now on the other foot and I would not have been at all surprised if we had been given a rough ride.

We need not have worried. Our reception on landing at Cape Town was akin to a heroes' return. Everyone appeared to be glad to see us, from cricket officials to journalists to the man in the street. The players, when we met them, were every bit as friendly, accepting us as part of their squad without even a hint of background bitterness.

I had signed for Western Province on a three-year contract, while still in South Africa on the SAB tour in March. John Emburey had not been offered terms until much later during the summer which he will remember with very mixed emotions. He had been hauled over the coals by his county, Middlesex, on his return from South Africa. It was a delicate situation – they were angry that he had not informed them of his part in the tour when the opportunity arose at a committee meeting just prior to our departure; John rightly pointed out that to have done so would have been to break the terms in his tour contract and possibly put the entire venture at risk. Middlesex, unrepentant, stripped him of the vice-captaincy and, in effect, made it virtually certain that he would not now be Mike Brearley's successor as skipper when he retired after the 1982 season. This was quite a blow to 'Embers', who has a shrewd cricketing brain and was ambitious to do the captain's job, but he overcame his disappointment to play a considerable part, with bat and ball, in Middlesex giving Brearley the perfect parting gift by running away with the County Championship, winning it by a 39-point margin.

John's terms with Western Province probably compared unfavourably with mine and when we were allocated to different clubs on our arrival, he certainly received the rough end of the deal. Part of the agreement was that our clubs should find us each appropriate accommodation, and while Claremont – to whom I was assigned – put Brenda and I in a comfortable flat in a pleasant area near the Newlands ground, John and Susie found themselves in a cramped, inconvenient and quite inadequate flat over some shops a mile or so away. His complaints were heeded, however, and fortunately he was moved into the next block to ours, so that the two girls could spend most of the time together while we were away playing.

Not, to be honest, that we were away all that much. Our commitment to Western Province involved eight Currie Cup matches of three-day duration, a floodlit league sponsored by Benson and Hedges, the one-day Nissan Shield knockout tournament and various inter-provincial challenge matches such as the Hunts Cup, in which WP traditionally play Eastern Province, and the Protea Challenge against Transvaal. But this by no means amounted to a full winter's employment, and, even allowing for club matches and coaching duties, there was a substantial amount of spare time. My weekly itinerary went something like this:

MONDAY Free by day. Evening fielding practice and training at Newlands.

TUESDAY Free morning. Afternoon game for Mobil XI against local school side. Evening coaching session at Claremont until 7 p.m.

WEDNESDAY Voluntary nets at Newlands in the morning. Free afternoon. Compulsory evening practice at Newlands for entire Western Province squad.

THURSDAY Free by day. Evening coaching at Claremont.

FRIDAY Free by day.

SATURDAY Club match for Claremont.

SUNDAY Free all day.

I have taken an example of the idlest sort of week, but these were not rare. Instead of Wednesday evening practice, we would sometimes have a match in the floodlit league which could entail a day of travelling and a night away. The Currie Cup games usually began on a Friday or Saturday but, on average, they would only occur once every three or four weeks. If you went away, however, the tendency was sometimes to play two matches on tour in close succession.

The club cricket is played over two Saturdays in Cape Town, but even this arrangement has elastic rules. For instance, if Claremont were due to begin a match one Saturday, and I knew I would be unavailable for the second Saturday due to a Currie Cup fixture, this did not preclude me from playing. I would simply be replaced by another player for the second week. This did seem to be an open invitation to sharp practice within the rules and, on one occasion during my second season with Claremont, the club pulled one of the most successful switches imaginable. We were playing against Northerns, a decent club side, and I knew I was only able to play the first Saturday. We batted first and made around 200, of which I scored 80, then we dismissed Northerns for 180. With 45 minutes play remaining I went in again and threw the bat at everything, hammering 75 in 12 overs before being out. On the concluding Saturday, I was substituted by a very capable opening bowler, who promptly took five for 20 to complete our win!

The full title of my club was Claremont Varsity Old Boys, which was an amalgamation of two clubs, both of whom had long been established in the leagues. Claremont had been through a bad time the season before I joined, which probably persuaded them to engage me, and it was a thrill for me as much as for their own members when I helped them win the league in 1982–83.

I was impressed by both the standard and the depth of club cricket. The big difference one must bear in mind when comparing it with English cricket, of course, is that in South Africa the first-class cricketers are able to play some club games which obviously raises the standard considerably. Claremont, however, ran eight teams, so everyone who wanted to play could find their own level, and on Tuesday and Thursday evenings there would invariably be 50 or 60 players at the ground for me to coach. My value to the club probably lay more in this direction, because my playing appearances were severely restricted by the majority of weekends being given over to a Western Province match of either one or three days.

My contract did not involve me in coaching schools, unlike the jobs which a number of our March touring side had taken. John Lever, for instance, had joined Les Taylor in Durban but, apart from playing for Natal, he also spent a good deal of time going round the local schools. The coaching system for schoolboys is extremely well organized in South Africa, with more than 50 English professionals flown out each year primarily to supervise the boys, and a number of contracted South African professionals going to schools each week as part of their regular duties. Schools play on good pitches, practice a good deal and learn fast. It makes the English schools system look a sorry mess.

Where I went to school, the master who took us for cricket had no ability at the game and no credentials to be coaching us. He was also very short on enthusiasm, and when he was not available or just failed to turn up, we didn't play. It was as simple as that. Cricket was considered unimportant, almost to the point of being a nuisance, and I know it is much the same in many other schools around the country. In South Africa, cricket is on the curriculum and the SACU put money into coaching the boys, because it is obviously in their future interests to do so. I fully appreciate that the make-up of the English first-class game simply does not allow professionals any time to coach at schools on anything like a regular basis, but surely this does not stop us making much more effort to improve the facilities in schools and their general attitude to the game, and perhaps introduce county cricketers to undertake a coaching circuit.

Although I was enjoying being paid well for a very good life,I did feel that some concessions in this direction should be made, which is why I played regularly for the Mobil XI on Tuesday afternoons. Mobil the oil company, put a great deal of money into the South African coaching system and one of the offshoots is this team, which happened to be captained and organized by Stuart Leary, who was director of coaching in the province and very much a Ken Barrington-type manager figure to the Western Province side. Each week, Stuart would take a capable team, including several of the WP squad and some strong club players, to a different school in the area. We would often include two or three African youngsters, and the success of the scheme could be judged by the reaction of the schoolboys, to whom it was a thrill, a challenge and a potential advancement in their game to come up against such relatively illustrious opposition. Stuart was insistent, and rightly so, that we should not mock the system by playing joke cricket and we all treated it fairly seriously. At its worst, it was a middle practice. At its best, it was competitive cricket with a cause.

I got on famously with Leary from the first time we met. South African-born, he had come to England to play soccer for Charlton Athletic and Queen's Park Rangers, and was also a very capable county cricketer for Kent. Approaching 50 by the time I went to Cape Town, he was still extremely active in the game, running the Western Province nets with impressive enthusiasm and cheerfully doing duties as our general factotum, baggageman and valet, quite apart from being our coach when we travelled away.

He had players in his care who were on a variety of contrasting contracts, and some who were not on contract at all. There are still a proportion of players in the Currie Cup who are not full-time professionals, and a few – like WP's leg-spinner Denys Hobson – who are playing as amateurs. Hobson is an accountant, fortunate enough to be a director of a company which permits him to go missing whenever he is wanted by WP. Our side probably had the largest number of full-timers in the country, with Peter Kirsten the captain, Stephen Jefferies, Garth le Roux, Kenny McEwan, Omar Henry, Emburey and myself. Apart from us and the amateurs, the third category involves young players who are contracted by the SACU to coach, and may play some provincial cricket as well.

The top professionals in the South African system are paid something similar to the county earnings of a leading player in England. The difference is that the South Africans have to play far fewer games to get their money. While I was there, there was some disquiet about the fact that Hobson, for instance, was missing out on the rewards despite having been part of the WP side for a number of years, and there was talk that the system could be changed to financially recognize the experienced, long-serving players no matter what their contractual status.

Every male in South Africa has to do his National Service stint and, when I went over in 1982, Steve Jefferies and Adrian Kuiper were still in the Navy. They were allowed leave from duties whenever WP wanted them – another indication of the nationwide importance of sport in South Africa – but, the combined Services ran a club side in the league which could sometimes be extremely formidable.

We settled into the routine surprisingly quickly in Cape Town. Brenda looked up some old friends and began to thoroughly enjoy herself. We ate well, laughed a lot, lived comfortably. But very soon the Currie Cup season began, something I looked upon as a new and demanding challenge in my career.

The first thing I discovered about provincial cricket in South Africa is that it can be cut-throat. The season is quite long, the number of matches to be played relatively small, so each game assumes great importance – far more significance, for instance, than virtually any County Championship fixture back in England. The Currie Cup is played over three days and the hours are longer than in England. Play starts at ten-thirty and continues until six-thirty and, if the start of the game is delayed by the weather for anything upwards of an hour, the second and third days will automatically start half-an-hour earlier, at ten o'clock. Unlike in England, where this starting time caused such problems in one-day cricket during 1982, any dew has cleared from the ground by ten and the sun is often quite hot.

As in England, South Africans play a bonus points system during the first innings of each side but, whereas County Championship bonus points are confined to four each for batting and bowling, in the Currie Cup they are potentially unlimited. If your team happens to score 550 in the first 85 overs of a match, you will reap a rich harvest of points.

I was struck by the response of the public in Cape Town. Cricket really is important to them – or, at least, winning at cricket is. Inter-provincial rivalry is very fierce and this partisan support evidently gets through to the players, who are made to feel they must win at virtually any cost. Some games, of course, mean more than others, but none mean as much as the Currie Cup confrontations with Transvaal.

Over the past few years, Western Province and Transvaal have vied for the title of South Africa's most powerful team. Whenever they meet, it seems, there is far more at stake than merely points, or even just prestige. It is the kind of occasion that Merseyside knows when Everton play Liverpool. There is no parallel in English county cricket. The atmosphere is electric, enough to make the most composed player a shade nervy and, if there is no needle on the field, there certainly will be in the crowd.

The Currie Cup season revolves around the meetings between these two sides and, to the cricket followers of Cape Town, a defeat against any other province is unthinkable, complete disaster. Even draws against the lesser opposition are only grudgingly accepted because it is essential to stay in touch with Transvaal in the league table until the time comes to play them again. WP's home match with Transvaal traditionally takes place over the New Year period and draws phenomenal crowds. In the years that I was involved, the ground would be packed with 15,000 people on the opening morning, and the other two days would bring in almost as many. These were bigger crowds than the four-day internationals against my English side could attract, and I was surprised by the depth of personal animosity in the stands. The Cape Town crowd hated

Transvaal's captain, Clive Rice, and loudly let it be known; the WP captain, Peter Kirsten, was equally unpopular when we went on the road.

In the 1982–83 season, we were beaten by Transvaal in Cape Town, and it was Garth le Roux who summed up the passions of the public when he said, only half-jokingly, 'That means a week in – it'll be dodgy going into the pubs until it dies down.' He didn't mean that we would actually have been in physical danger, but there is no doubt in my mind that we would have come in for some animated abuse if we had ventured near too many of our supporters in the immediate aftermath of defeat. They don't take kindly to it in South Africa.

Despite losing the big one that winter, we did well enough against the other sides to finish second in the points table and so qualify for the Currie Cup final, which is played over four days and in which, inevitably, we would once again be facing Transvaal. The fact that the result was no different this time round in no way influences my view that this is an unfair method of deciding the competition. It may well be that one province is overwhelmingly superior to all rivals during the eight fixtures played on a league basis yet still loses the cup through one below-par performance in the sudden-death final.

I can appreciate the reasons for organizing it this way, however. By including a final, they were guaranteeing that the season would come to a recognizable crescendo, attractive to the media, to the public and – probably, most important in the eyes of the SACU – attractive to their sponsors. The South African Breweries group, who also sponsored our tour, were good and generous sponsors who appeared to have the game at heart. But that does not mean they were willing to pass up the best available advertising outlet, which is obviously what a nationally-televised final would provide.

It seems SAB were not entirely content with this arrangement, though, because for my second winter in Cape Town the system was altered again. Now, we had only to play each of our four opponents (Transvaal, Northern Transvaal, Natal and Eastern Province) once. The team standing bottom of the five-strong table then dropped out and the cup was decided by two semi-finals and a final involving the top four sides. From our own point of view there was a serious flaw in this method because, although we played well in the league matches and finished top of the table, entitling us to a semi-final against the fourth-placed side Eastern Province, we were for some odd reason obliged to play them away from home. And we very nearly lost. Our neighbours had a second-innings target of only around 160 for a victory which would have been cited as a catastrophe back in Cape Town. Life would not have been worth living for some while, if Steve Jefferies had not summoned his most effective swing-bowling form to dismiss them cheaply and save our faces. But it was no surprise to anyone when we found ourselves up against Transvaal again in the final, and the result was maddeningly similar to the previous year.

I could pay no higher tribute to Transvaal than to say they are probably the best team I have ever faced outside Test cricket. Western Australia, in the heyday of Dennis Lillee and Rod Marsh, were a formidable unit; Barbados have often boasted a near Test-strength side in the Shell Shield in West Indies. But Transvaal hardly included a single player who would have looked out of place in the international arena, and their batting, with Jimmy Cook, Alvin Kallicharran, Graeme Pollock and Rice, the captain, leading the way, was simply fearsome to bowl against.

Surprisingly, they attracted nothing like the level of support given to Western Province. There are few better places in the world to play or watch cricket than The Wanderers ground in Johannesburg, but there is not the same feeling for cricket there as exists in Cape Town and, but for the most major games, the Transvaal crowds are poor. Cup and Nissan Shield matches are all on provincial television anyway, which might be said to deter people from going to the grounds, but the games are so much more of an event than English county games, for instance, that it would seem strange if they were not televised.

With the exception of Transvaal, I did not think the standard of cricket was very much different to decent county level. South Africans, however, are by nature aggressive people and their cricket certainly matched the image. No quarter was asked or given on the field, and the umpires – who were generally very inferior to their

English counterparts – came under an incessant verbal attack from some players as a kind of psychological warfare.

The social life associated with first-class cricket sides there is much the same as it is in England. When the team is playing away, the old familiar syndrome of bars-restaurants-hotel which, I know, has driven some cricketers out of the game, was very much apparent. South Africans are sociable and gregarious; most of the team enjoy the proverbial few beers, and the presence of John Emburey and I in their midst had no effect at all on the WP side – we were never made to feel unpopular, unwanted, or anything except part of the set-up.

'Embers' was outstandingly successful during our first season with the province, taking almost 40 wickets in the Currie Cup and proving, to any who still doubted after his injury-interrupted tour early in 1982, that he is among the finest off-break bowlers in the world. He also bowled extremely well in the Benson and Hedges night cricket competition, which was more of a surprise to everyone because spin was hardly used at all in this form of cricket.

The floodlit game depends entirely on climate for its success. It can be played very effectively in Australia because, although it gets dark quite early, the nights are warm and seldom wet; the same applies in South Africa. In an English high-summer, darkness does not fall until around ten o'clock, which makes a nonsense of using lights at all, and if you try to play the games in early spring and late autumn you are asking for trouble with bad weather. Those experiments which have taken place in our country have almost all been on football grounds, where the short, square boundaries bias the game too heavily in favour of the bat and, although a match between Essex and West Indies some years ago drew a big crowd to the Chelsea ground, it was very much joke cricket even before the heavens opened to add a touch of farce.

Night cricket in South Africa is big business, however. The colourful spectacle and the exciting atmosphere have caught the imagination of the public – quite probably a different public to that which would come to see a three-day game, but a substantial following nonetheless. The league is essentially small, containing only the five major provinces, as in the Currie Cup, but at the conclusion of the four-match round-robin there are semi-finals and a final. Lights are now being built on the main Kingsmead ground in Durban but, in my time with Western Province, home night matches were played at a multi-purpose stadium in Green Point. To conform to regulations regarding minimum distances to the boundary, the playing area extended outside a tartan athletics track, which was no real problem, and a cycle-track, which was. Like most cycle-racing circuits, it was built on a camber, which meant that a fielder, chasing a high hit which landed on the slope of the cycle-track, could suffer the unusual fate of seeing the ball, while still in play, rebound crazily over his head.

We also had an artificial wicket, which set us apart from the other provinces, most of whom were able to play on their own grounds – lights, for instance, existed at The Wanderers and made for a magical night-time setting. At Green Point, however, scores were invariably very high and often rather false, but the balance was not exclusively held by the batsman and 'Embers' showed what a talented thoughtful spinner could do to keep the total in check. All the provinces were allocated a colour for their night cricket clothes. We had to wear royal blue. White balls were used, and the crowds flocked in. There were never fewer than 12,000 to watch our home games, and when Transvaal were the visitors the ground was bulging with 20,000 inside. There was a good deal of razzmatazz in the style of American football; the provinces each had their own catchy song, like 'Come on Aussie, Come on' ditty which was so popular during World Series Cricket, and at the fall of wickets, or any other high points of the match, these would blare out across the grounds on the public address system. Traditionalists might well have hated it all, but I confess I found it quite stimulating, so long as it was not confused with the real thing.

We had some very competitive matches, none better than a home game against Eastern Province at Green Point in which the visitors scored 299 in their 45 overs and still lost. My most vivid and alarming memory of the floodlit competition, however, is of a match at Berea Park, Pretoria against Northern Transvaal. To appease a large crowd, we were playing on through heavy rain and I was fielding at the top end of the ground. The rain was clearly about to develop into a humdinger of a storm and, as the first forks of lightning slashed across the ground, I glanced up and, to my horror, realised I was fielding directly underneath an electricity pylon. I did not stay there much longer.

One of the most encouraging features of my two winters in Cape Town was the very definite, if gradual, advances made by coloured cricketers. The African blacks, not to be confused, were still very much keener on soccer and their own teams, such as the Kaiser Chiefs and Morocco Swallows, lived up to their spectacular names with some very entertaining football, much of which was televised. In cricket, however, the coloured population was making progress under the tuition of British coaches such as Paul Phillipson, of Sussex, and Kevin Lyons, then of Glamorgan, who spent a lot of time travelling into the townships to encourage, correct and cajole. Coloureds were steadily becoming more integrated in the previously all-white clubs, but the Africans did have their own side in the Cape Town league. They were known as Langa, and they had built their own home ground and I was invited along to speak at the opening of the pavilion, of which they were plainly proud.

If this acceptance and development was necessarily slow it was a great stride forward from what had gone before. Those who decry South Africa, mentioning sport in the same breath as politics, tend to sweep aside the positive statements which could be made about the country's efforts – even if they are generally confined to the sporting scene – and this is terribly unfair on so many people who have devoted much of their lives in recent years to putting some injustices to right. I would certainly name Joe Pamensky among this number and I came to respect him as a fair-minded man – ambitious, but willing to spare no effort to promote South African cricket as a multi-racial sport. He wanted people to accept, all around the cricket world, the strides which had been made to break down the apartheid barriers. But very few listened. So eventually he and his SACU body took the matter into their own hands. If the ICC and its member countries insisted on shutting their eyes and ears to everything that had been improved in South Africa, consistently refusing even to hear their case, much less to send an cxperimental touring team (which was all they asked for), then they would use the vastly impressive commercial support available to them and find their own international opposition. We were the first to go, but the two teams who came out after us were personally risking more and, from South Africa's viewpoint, achieving more, for the simple reason that they were black.

The visit by a Sri Lankan team had very little impact on the South African public, probably a great deal more on the outside world. They may not have amounted to much on a scale of possible international opposition but the very fact that an Asian side had been tempted to go there at all was a painful slap in the face for many political agitators who love nothing more than to use cricket as a pawn in their propaganda war against policies which sportsmen can do nothing about. If the Sri Lankans had not broken the ice I very much doubt if the West Indian side which followed them out could have been persuaded to go.

In purely cricket terms, I thought the disappointment of the Sri Lankan series was the somersault in the career of Ajit de Silva. When England played in their country early in 1982, de Silva was by some distance their best bowler; experienced and controlled, his left-arm spin caused us considerable problems and his four victims in the Inaugural Test in Colombo were Tavaré, Fletcher, Emburey and myself. I thought he was quite a capture for the unofficial squad which went to South Africa, but de Silva's bowling was in one of those inexplicable slumps which seem chiefly to plague spinners of his type. He began to deliver head-high full-tosses and double-bouncers more regularly than he hit a good length, until eventually it became embarrassing to him and the rest of his team.

The West Indians, under Lawrence Rowe, were predictably a much bigger hit with the public, and for the first time I think the blacks and coloureds in the crowd felt they had an identity with the matches that they were seeing. Eventually, I fancy some of them might have ended up supporting the West Indians but the important thing was that they were there and enjoying it.

Rowe's players knew they had a great deal to lose. Those who came from Guyana or Jamaica could never go home again because of the uproar their tour had caused and the stigma which was forever to remain attached to them; the other islands were more forgiving than this, but every player who went was banned for life from West Indian Test and domestic cricket.

The accusation that they amounted only to a West Indian B team could only be partly justified. Alvin Kallicharran remained one of the finest batsmen in the world and would certainly have commanded a place in the Test team if he had not chosen to play for Transvaal and risk a ban; Faoud Bacchus, David Murray, Colin Croft and Sylvester Clarke had all been in the West Indian Test team during their tour of Australia the previous winter, while the unpredictable Collis King was one of the most effective limited-overs cricketers the world has seen. The rest of the party were by no means mugs at this level and, if the rumoured arrival of Malcolm Marshall and Desmond Haynes had actually transpired, the official West Indian side would have been left with a lot of holes to fill.

South Africa, their great names growing old and staving off retirement only for the incentive of the opposition they had awaited so long, struggled. This, to an outsider such as myself, seemed good for them as for so many years they had buoyed up their spirits by imagining they must be the best even if they had no way of measuring it. They can be arrogant, superior . . . and defeat did much to bring them back down to earth.

I was never able to understand the reluctance of West Indies to play Clarke regularly and it was probably frustration which prompted him to take up the South African offer. I doubt if he has any regrets. He became a hero among the coloured population and was regarded in awe by the whites. Transvaal signed him during that first tour and his presence, I am afraid, made them invincible rather than merely formidable. Bacchus also went into the Currie Cup, taking my place in the Western Province side for the winter of 1984–85.

The major problem the South Africans encountered with the West Indians was one of temperament. There was a good deal of bickering over money, and a certain amount of indiscipline which only emphasised the extraordinarily fine job Clive Lloyd has done in moulding his official side, with all its contrasting backgrounds and temperaments, into an efficient and well-behaved unit.

The opening night match on the West Indians' schedule in 1983

–84 was on the point of chaos when the tourists refused to take the field until a dispute over payments and terms was resolved. They eventually shambled out in a concoction of gear, King wearing the officially designated red strip, most of the others in all white. It was not an impressive sight and I don't think it did much for their image. On another occasion, the starting time of a game had to be put back because the West Indian team had not arrive at the ground. Their excuse was simple enough. Most of the players had overslept!

Despite these minor trials, the tours were thought of as successes and the public turned out to watch in enormous numbers. The South Africans were thereafter content to sit back for a time and let the world consider the significance of what had happened. Against all the odds, they had staged international series against cricketers from three different countries, and staged them with verve and efficiency. The crowds had been black, brown and white and, if the South African side remained an all-white affair, it was only a matter of time before the coaching schemes produced a coloured star. They had much on which to congratulate themselves, even if nobody else would do it for them.

As for me, I came home from my second winter with Western Province having told them I would not be going back. This had nothing to do with any lack of enjoyment on my part – quite the opposite was true, in fact – but there were things I had to do in England. Essex had granted me a benefit in 1985, which looked as if it might be a big year for me in more than one way. A winter at home, I thought, was called for.

9

Champions and comedians

Just before the 1983 English season got underway, Surrey captain Roger Knight unwittingly put fire in the bellies of everyone at Essex. Interviewed on a London television station, and asked to give his thoughts on the county competitions ahead, Knight made the great mistake of saying that Essex were a spent force. He thought too many of our better players had grown old together and that we would be unable to maintain a challenge in the Championship.

If any more incentive was needed to help us prove that 1982 had been a brief and unrepresentative barren spell, this was it. To put slightly new words to an old saying, there is no team like a team scorned. Roger was not the only person eager to write us off as being 'over the hill' – I noticed that the bookmakers were offering very attractive odds against us winning the title, and I flirted with the idea of becoming a gambler – but, the more times we heard it said, the more determined we all became to disprove the theory.

'Fletch', coming up to his thirty-ninth birthday and doubtless among those regarded as being past their best, was very evidently irritated by this slur on his side and wasted no time in telling us what was expected. I don't think we let him down. The championship pennant returned to Chelmsford after four years' absence, and we came close, agonisingly close, to bringing home the Benson and Hedges Cup as well.

To be fair to Roger Knight, who is an underrated cricketer, the evidence of the previous summer, plus the ages of many of our squad, meant there was more than a little justification for his remarks. It was not just a sweeping slander. After all, the five bowlers who had borne most of the load in recent years were all in their mid-thirties or older and could not realistically be expected to show the stamina or the penetration of a few seasons earlier. Roger was perhaps not to know Keith Fletcher's views that, in Neil Foster and Derek Pringle, he possessed the two best young seam bowlers in the country and that, to add a competitive edge to the batting department, two or three players of striking ability – among them Chris Gladwin and Paul Prichard – were almost ready to challenge for places. So yes, we had some older players, but we also had some high-quality replacements.

We were also lucky in that we were virtually free of disruption by England calls. Pringle was disregarded by England throughout 1983 after a disappointing tour of Australia, where he suffered substantial problems with bowling no-balls, not cured until well into the home season, and possibly did himself no good by failing to camouflage the apparent indifference and casualness which are his natural traits by a few more positive gestures. But, as I have already said, Test cricket came to him too easily and too quickly; a summer spent mostly in county cricket made him a better cricketer and certainly made us a better side.

Foster was a bonus, the size of which none of us can logically have expected when the season began. His career had been launched in the fairy-tale manner and almost ended as a horror story. He was only 18, and still at school, when he answered an SOS to come to Ilford and make his Championship debut in 1980. The papers understandably made much of this, interviewing everyone in sight including his school headmaster, and when the fuss had died down it was clear that we had an exceptional fast-bowling prospect. By the start of the 1982 season, Foster had physically filled out, added on a yard or two of pace and had begun to look every inch the part. 'Fletch' was very keen on him and went so far as to be quoted on a prediction that he would very soon play for England.

He was right, but in the meantime Neil went through a nightmare, his back breaking down completely just after he forced his way into the Championship side. He needed an operation and the insertion of plates to strengthen the spine, and he could do no more than watch from the pavilion for the rest of that summer. Steady work during the close-season, however, restored him to fitness and, if he had lost a shade of pace, his classical action and control of length and line still made him a very useful bowler to have in the squad. In 12 Championship matches during the summer of 1983 he picked up 51 wickets and, when Graham Dilley was forced by injury to withdraw from England's squad for the First Test against New Zealand, 'Fozzy' was dramatically called up, having just made a big impression on captain Bob Willis in a county game at Nuneaton.

Although he did not play at The Oval, he did get a game at Lord's, bowling well enough, though without any great success, and at the end of the season he was named in the tour party to go to New Zealand and Pakistan. It was an astonishing advance in the space of a few months for a young man who had started the season naturally nervous of whether his back would stand up to full-time cricket again, and reflected great credit not just on Neil for his fortitude but on the men connected with our club who had first nursed him back to full health and then shown the necessary confidence to play him.

Foster and Pringle made our seam attack the best in England. With John Lever, still tireless and ageless as our spearhead, 'Nobby' Phillip and Stuart Turner, we had a high-quality quintet of bowlers and, plainly, a very competitive situation as we could never play all five. It could be argued that Notts had, on paper, a better attack with Rice, Hadlee and Hendrick, but in 1983 Rice was never fit enough to bowl at all and Hadlee spent almost all summer with the touring New Zealanders. Middlesex, with their all-black trio of Wayne Daniel, Norman Cowans and Neil Williams, commanded respect but our attack had more variety and, I think, more reliability.

Only a decade earlier, it would have been unthinkable for Essex to have the healthy problem of needing to leave out a couple of fast bowlers in each game. Until 1973 the club only contracted 12 full-time professionals and I assume they were expected to stay fit. The occasional crises were dealt with by calling up ex-players or amateurs from the local clubs. Before I joined the club, we found ourselves a man short for a John Player League match in Somerset and Doug Insole, then approaching 50 and long since retired, was recruited. He drove all the way down to Weston-super-Mare only to be run out without facing a ball!

Nowadays, one of the secrets of the Essex success is a squad system which gives capable cover for every conceivable emergency. In 1982, when Foster broke down, 'Nobby' Phillip rose to the occasion with his best-ever season for us; the following year, when Neil was wanted by England, 'Nobby' came back into the side and bowled so well that we won two matches which might easily have slipped away. This is just one example of our back-up. Ken McEwan had a phenomenally successful 1983, scoring more than 2,000 runs with eight centuries. But, whenever he failed, the unsung heroes, such as Brian 'Lager' Hardie (1042 runs) or Keith Pont (802), would be around to shore up the innings.

I would add two further factors to explain Essex's recent glories. The first of these is Keith Fletcher, the most experienced captain in the game, a fine tactician for whom we all have nothing but respect. The second is the atmosphere which runs right through the club, from chairman to groundstaff. The committee never put the players under any unfair pressure; the players, by return, give their all. Everyone wants to win, but nobody wants to lose sight of the fact that it is, after all, only a game.

Success has not changed the people within the club. We are certainly more professional than we used to be and the fact that we have achieved so much means that we go onto the field expecting to win. But prima donnas are not tolerated and any bickering within the dressing-room is rapidly resolved. The great thing is, we all get on well together. I have known teams firmly split into three or four cliques, with individuals barely on speaking terms, and I fail to understand how they can maintain the right spirit in what is essentially a team game. Thank heavens, Essex have always, in my time, been a team on and off the field, and we have had the priceless bonus of some natural comedians to keep us all in the right frame of mind.

There are some players, Derek Randall for instance, whose antics on the field never fail to amuse a crowd but whose shy personality in the dressing-room does not match the comic image. Similarly, there are those who are forever telling stories and plotting practical jokes in the dressing-room yet, once on the field, become intense and withdrawn. Very few contrive to be funny in every situation without compromising their playing ability, but Ray East has always had the gift. There are those who will say that his clowning cost him honours, and I can believe it is true, because jokes on the field are not always guaranteed to endear a player to the authorities. But Ray rightly considered cricketers to be entertainers, and I can think of no one in the game whose character has been so enjoyed by the public who pay to watch.

There were times, of course, when Raymond clowned at the wrong moment and there was the odd occasion when 'Fletch' and he had words about it. But these were uncommon occurrences. For the most part, his humour was appreciated by all as a bonus when we were winning and a refreshing shaft of light when we were not.

Ray officially retired after the 1983 season. Given his own way, he would probably have quit midway through the year, but the club rightly persuaded him to stay on, probably hoping that he would change his mind. He was eager to coach and captain the second team, and he played the occasional first-team match in 1984 when injury robbed us of David Acfield, but enthusiasm for the seven-days-a-week routine of the county game had gone from him. Quite simply, he had had enough cricket.

Like most natural comedians, Ray is a complicated, moody man behind the joking front. There were times when he became deeply morose and disillusioned about life in general and cricket in particular, and yet I don't for a moment suppose he will be remembered for that. His epitaph will be the stories he created, stories which have become bar-room legends around the cricket circuit. Cricketers swap Ray East experiences rather as some people swap Irish jokes, and they can be equally absurd.

Probably the most famous of all dates back a number of years to a game against Lancashire at a time when their opening attack was the Test combination of Peter Lever and Ken Shuttleworth. Both were fine bowlers, but Raymond believed 'Shutt' was a little gullible, so decided to put his theory to the test. He went into bat with 'Shutt' bowling particularly well – fast, hostile and picking up wickets regularly. As Ray walked past him at the end of his run, he said quietly that he did not intend to hold things up and that so long as 'Shutt' pitched the ball up another wicket was as good as his. The first delivery, sure enough, was off full length and aimed to hit middle and off-stump but, with full flow of the bat, Ray played a crashing straight drive for four. Poor old Ken was predictably furious and it did not need great intellect to assess what was in his mind now. He raced in for the next ball but, even as the intended fierce bouncer left his hand, Raymond upstaged him by flinging his bat to one side and diving melodramatically to the other, finally lying flat out on the pitch as the ball passed harmlessly over his head.

At around the time of this particular piece of slapstick, Robin Hobbs, the leg-spinner, was still playing for us. A lanky, talkative character, Hobbs was the perfect foil for East and, indeed, they formed a very funny terrible trio with John Lever. I can vividly remember one dull session at Leyton being enlivened by an incident which revolved around Robin's fielding. He would usually field at cover, where he was very athletic and sometimes spectacular, but we ribbed him endlessly about the fact he could only stop the ball with his right hand. He was in his regular position on this day, and, when the ball was struck firmly to his right, he dived, scooped it up in his right hand, rolled over and got to his feet, in one continuous flowing movement. The crowd's applause for this splendid piece of fielding was still ringing out as Robin started the ball on its way back to the bowler, lobbing it to Ray at extra-cover. Then the East wit took over. Instead of catching it and ferrying it onwards in the normal fashion, he dived towards the ball, caught it, rolled on the ground, got up and threw it on to John at mid-off, who proceeded to go through exactly the same act. It is the type of spontaneous humour which never transmits well to paper or even to repetition, but we were all convulsed with laughter at the time.

Although Ray had a repertoire of histrionics with his bowling, most of the famous tales associated with him emanate from his batting. We were in trouble at Portsmouth one year, having followed on against Hampshire. Andy Roberts, the great West Indian, was nearing the end of his county career and needed some motivation to turn in his best efforts at that level, but the Hampshire skipper Bob Stephenson had apparently promised him a match off if he could bowl us out again and finish the match inside two days. This was enough for Andy, and we were rapidly six wickets down and heading for an apparently inevitable innings defeat. Ray went in at number eight and was soon fending off some violent lifters as

Roberts strained to finish us off. One smacked him on the glove and looped towards first slip, where David Rock plunged forward, picked it up low down and claimed the catch. Raymond was uncertain that the ball had carried and waited for the decision. Umpire Bill Alley, to everyone's surprise, gave him 'not out' and the game continued with A. M. E. Roberts fuming. Ray managed to get a single and scuttle up the other end, taking off his glove to rub the bruise as he did so. When he got there, Bill Alley demanded to know why he was massaging his hand. 'He hit me on the glove, Bill,' replied Ray.

'But I gave you not out – why didn't you walk?' protested the umpire.

'He didn't catch it cleanly, did he?'

'Yes he did . . . I thought it had hit you on the arm!'

This conversation at the non-striker's stumps might have been no more than an amusing aftermath to a misunderstanding, something to be repeated at a safe distance of time over a drink in the bar, but for the fact that every word of it was overheard by Mr Roberts.

To say he was not pleased is to understate the case more than a little. Ray knew precisely what to expect next time he was on the receiving end and he elected to take no chances. As Roberts climaxed his steaming approach with that classical delivery, fired now by anger as well as impatience, Raymond stepped away towards square leg and retreated rapidly and gratefully as the stumps were splayed.

It was another umpiring decision on a claimed catch which led to my favourite among all the Ray East stories. This one occurred during the 1983 season when we were playing at Tunbridge Wells. It was mid-June, the World Cup was in full swing elsewhere in the country and the sun was beating down as so often it seems to on this loveliest of all the Kent grounds. Approaching lunch-time, on I think the second day, Ray was once again batting. He played a ball off his legs into the mid-wicket area, where a perfectly simple catch was taken, but Ray stayed, waiting for the umpire to decide whether it had been a 'bump ball' or not. Jack van Geloven, the former Leicestershire player who has since retired from the first-class list to concentrate on running a pub in Yorkshire, considered for only a moment before raising his finger to give Ray out. 'Eastie', half in jest, threw his arms wide before leaving the field along with the rest of the players as lunch had been called.

All through the interval, Ray was baiting poor Jack, questioning him time and again about whether he wanted to change his mind and rule that it had, after all, been a 'bump ball'. Jack of course declined and, donning his white coat again, walked back to the middle at the head of the fielding side. David East was due in at number nine, but Ray had not had his fill of fun yet. Stopping his namesake from leaving the dressing-room, Ray put on his pads and gloves again, added a helmet with a visor and marched back to the wicket with our other not out batsman. The Kent fielders were by this time in fits of laughter (Ray's walk is very recognizable even when he is hiding his face behind a visor!) but Jack was blissfully oblivious to what was going on until Ray reached the middle, turned to the umpire and asked: 'You did say it was a "bump ball" Jack, didn't you?'

I have never seen an umpire jump in the air in fright as Jack did then. Ray was dispatched back to the pavilion, having given everyone a good and harmless laugh with one of his finest-ever performances.

Ray did not collect his usual quota of wickets in 1983, chiefly because the seamers were entrusted with most of the bowling. But if this influenced his decision to quit, as I think it did, it was nothing to the situation in 1979, when 'J.K.' had taken 60-plus wickets by the end of June, our first Championship title was already an odds-on bet and our two spinners had hardly bowled at all. East and Acfield were nicknamed 'sweater-carrier' and 'sawdust-getter' and, entering into the joke, they would salute everyone they met with two fingers raised in the fast bowlers' grip and solemnly say: 'Seam, brother'.

David Acfield is of markedly different background to everyone else in our side, yet he fits perfectly into the pattern of things. He went to Brentwood public school and Cambridge University, where he won a Blue for fencing – a sport in which he later became a British champion and an Olympic international – as well as for cricket. Although we have a more recent Cambridge graduate in our side, Acfield and Pringle are no more alike than salt and pepper.

David is of the old school: blazers and ties will be worn, physical training will be hated but endured. Considering that he would probably have been far better suited by the Essex side of the 1950s and 1960s he has adapted remarkably well. He plays up to his image of the schoolteacher with the posh accent, but has a dry humour all of his own.

Inevitably, he receives at least his share of the leg-pulling in the dressing-room and he has not been allowed to forget the scene when he dislocated a finger when dropping a catch at Ilford during the 1984 season. He ran around, as one of our players observed, like a headless chicken, waving his hand above his head in distress signals – and as usually happens in our side when someone gets an injury which has its humorous side – received no sympathy whatsoever for weeks afterwards.

There was a fear during 1983 that 'Accers' might join his spin partner and good friend Raymond out at grass. He is a nervous man, often unhappy when we are away from home for long periods, and I think he probably felt that, like Ray, he had been playing long enough. Thankfully, he changed his mind – I hope David is around for a good few years yet as he is a distinct and unmistakable character in a game where too many players look and behave the same.

We did not regain the Championship without an epic struggle with Middlesex in 1983, and from a cricket point of view it was entirely right and proper that these two counties, commonly acknowledged to be the best around, should be fighting out the most important of the four titles right up to the final game of the long season. But we also came face to face with Middlesex in the final of the Benson and Hedges Cup, and this time we came off second best. It would, however, be much more accurate to say that we lost the game rather than that Middlesex won it, because that July day at Lord's our performance embodied all that has been worst about Essex cricket over the years – we got ourselves into a virtually invincible position and then simply threw it all away.

Only three days previously we had given a dress rehearsal. Playing Kent in the second round of the NatWest Bank Trophy, we were set a forbidding target of 275 but looked to be cruising. I made 122, possibly my best innings all summer. It seemed we had only to complete the formalities when I got out to a tired and, as it turned out, rash shot. We ended up being beaten by four runs and I never thought I would see a collapse like it again.

I was wrong. At Lord's, our target was very much more comfortable. We had to make 197 in 55 overs after a fine bowling performance, especially by Neil Foster. Still feeling the benefit of my hundred against Kent, I set off at great pace and was very annoyed to get an edge to a ball from Neil Williams when four short of 50. But we were 79 for one, well ahead of the clock. It was a good start. Although the pace dropped, we looked in no great danger when the second wicket fell at 127 and, despite a few more alarms, we were able to reach 185 for five, needing only 12 to win with half the side left.

We will never know whether we were psyched out of it by the still fresh memory of the Kent fiasco, or whether this was an entirely new nightmare. But the fact is that we lost those last five wickets for only seven runs, Norman Cowans bowling Neil Foster with the first ball of the final over to give the capacity crowd a sensational finish that the majority, being Essex supporters, could well have done without.

There were a lot of long faces in our changing-room that night, and quite a few looked frankly disbelieving. Once was bad enough, but to lose twice in that fashion in the space of four days, eliminating ourselves from both the knockout competitions, was almost too much to bear. The party, planned for us whether we won or lost, took some while to get into swing.

We did have a hero that day, however, despite the fact that he took only one wicket and did not score a single run. By all medical logic, John Lever should not have been on the field at all, as only a few days earlier he had undergone an emergency operation for a stomach condition which – the doctors solemnly assured him – was potentially fatal. John had begun to feel rough during Southend week and was understandably worried by the pus, evidently poison, emitting from his stomach. He had no idea quite how serious this could be, and it was only through the insistence of our physio, Ray Cole, that he went to consult a specialist. Within hours he was being operated upon, and he was later told that he might have had only hours to live if the poison had entered the bloodstream.

If he was not quite at his best in the final it had to be accepted that it was little short of a miracle he was playing at all. The surgery did clear up the complaint, although he suffered a slight recurrence 12 months later, but considering the drama of it all it was a calculated risk to include him in the side, and underlined Keith Fletcher's absolute faith in the ability of his number one bowler.

This loyalty has a long and well-justified history. Ever since Keith took over as captain, 'J.K.' has been an automatic choice as new-ball bowler and if, like all of us, he has had the occasional bad match, he has never had a bad season and, more than once, he has been quite the outstanding individual in the country. That was surely the case in 1983 when, quite apart from the abdominal problems which meant him missing out on a game or two and not being fully fit for others, he also suffered a broken toe, yet still managed to take 106 wickets in, effectively, two-thirds of the season.

As a team, however, we still had much to do if we were to take anything tangible from the season after the sacrifice of the two one-day competitions. Even the most naturally buoyant of sides, a category into which we usually fall, can have their confidence shaken by two such performances in rapid succession and we had to remind ourselves of the more agreeable days of an already memorable season. None was likely to linger in the mind longer than the late May Monday afternoon at Chelmsford when we bowled out Surrey for 14.

The opening day of the game had been entirely lost to rain and, with the atmosphere heavy and humid, I have no doubt 'Fletch' was anxious to win the toss and insert. He lost it, however, and Roger Knight – whose comments only weeks beforehand were still fresh in our memories – set his bowlers to work. Every trick in the day went to us, thereafter, 'Fletch' scoring a very fine century to prove that one old man, at least, was not over the hill, before 'Nobby' Phillip illustrated that he could still bowl a bit, too. Knight lbw b Phillip 0, was one of the more satisfying dismissals in an incredible flurry of six ducks. 'Nobby' finished the innings with the remarkable figures of six for four, Foster being relatively expensive with four for ten! Any smugness we felt at this was rapidly muted when Surrey batted out the final day to claim the draw, Knight being unbeaten with 101, but we felt we had proved a point to him, nonetheless.

Four successive crushing wins during June and early July (two by an innings, one by nine wickets, the other by 201 runs) kept us well in touch with Middlesex, who were winning their games equally as easily. We then suffered one of those inexplicable bad patches leading up to the aberrations against Kent and at Lord's. We lost by ten wickets to Warwickshire at Nuneaton and then by four wickets to Hampshire, who scored 410 in the fourth innings after being completely outplayed over the previous two days. In both those defeats, significantly, we were missing 'J.K.', and when he was restored to the team the points began to flow again. The tape was in sight when we overhauled Middlesex but the issue was still not settled as we went into our respective final matches – Middlesex playing Notts at Trent Bridge while we met Yorkshire at home.

This was to be a momentous weekend at Chelmsford as, on the Sunday, a complete wash out handed the John Player League title to Yorkshire and we were treated to the sight of hundreds of their supporters (some behaving suspiciously like the followers of Leeds United) gathered in front of our pavilion in the pouring rain to cheer Ray Illingworth. There was not much more cheering in their county during the winter ahead and Illingworth was eventually to be among the casualties as the coup by the Boycott camp ousted the old committee and held the cricket headlines for weeks on end.

To most of us in the game, Yorkshire are a people apart and it is sad to see a county which was once the greatest in cricket confine its activities to undignified public bickering. It is not for me to take sides, or even to suggest which of the distinct arguments might have right on its side. All I know is that to have been a player at Yorkshire while this war has raged must have been purgatory, and the whole affair has made me even more appreciative of the surroundings and the atmosphere in which I have been lucky enough to play all my county cricket.

Two days later, the Schweppes Championship was ours. The weather made it all something of an anti-climax, both our game and that at Trent Bridge ending in stalemate, but it was enough to ensure we held on to our lead, and enough to justify the discomfort I put myself through in making my third Championship hundred of the year. The pitch was green, made to suit the seamers. I did not go in on the Saturday evening because I broke my finger in the field, but I went in on the Monday, at the fall of the fourth wicket, and it was one of my best efforts of the season to guide the side from a perilous 58 for four to 288 and a first-innings lead of 84.

I had been heavily outscored in three-day cricket that summer by my close friend Ken McEwan, by now a team-mate in Cape Town as well as at Chelmsford. Kenny is a quiet, restrained character, utterly untypical of his race, and a player of sometimes languid elegance for whom nothing ever seems to demand any effort. Where I will strike the ball, Kenny will coax it; the contrast has been an effective one for Essex over the years.

My own best innings had come in one-day cricket and, until mid-August, I had not even scored a century in the Championship. I still suffered motivation problems and I knew that my concentration was not always what it should have been. Now and again, especially during the World Cup, my thoughts did stray towards playing for England. I had one more summer of suspension. And I resolved to make the best of it.

10

1984: annus mirabilis

A cricketer can always look back on all kinds of turning points in his career. But I have no doubt what has made me the player I am today – and it is all due to my wife Brenda's Auntie Grace.

I have never had any particular mentors, either in county or Test cricket. When things have gone wrong and the runs have refused to come, I have usually worked out the problems and the cures myself, sooner or later. But on the Australian tour of 1978–79 I was baffled by my loss of form, and it was Auntie Grace who unwittingly put me right.

Mike Brearley had dropped me down the order from one to four in a bid to keep me away from the new ball and perhaps bring the best out of me. But it didn't work. I am convinced I would have lost my Test place if Clive Radley had not taken a fearful blow on the head in a state game, draining all his confidence to a point where he was virtually discounted. Even then, I only hung on by making twenties and thirties and, despite the delight of beating the Aussies 5–1 on their own soil, I came home wondering what could be done to put things right.

Then Auntie Grace got involved. It transpired that she had been videoing the highlights of the Test series as they appeared on the BBC news programmes. She gave me the full tape and, one spring evening in 1979, I sat down to view it with the specific idea of finding out if there was anything which looked consistently amiss with my game.

There was. I squirmed as I watched it. They say the camera cannot lie but it was now showing me some pictures I had not expected to see, and suddenly the lessons of the tour failures became all too clear and I knew exactly why I had not made an appropriate contribution to our victory. Virtually every time I faced, I was alarmed to watch myself getting square-on, my chest turning to face the bowler as he delivered. I was also getting too far across the crease and my head, instead of remaining straight and still, was plunging into my chest. My whole upper body became contorted into a crouch position and, thinking back through each innings and relating my inner thoughts of the moment to the pictures I was now witnessing, it was perfectly clear that, the more I gritted my teeth and concentrated, the more I crouched and the worse my predicament would become.

At the time, out there in the heat and the tension of an Ashes series, I had been at a loss to work out why I was consistently getting out lbw. The video made it all clear. I don't think a batsman is ever certain how far across his stumps he is moving, because part of the movement is instinctive and sub-conscious, but I had begun to look perfectly horrible – and it needed technical aid in the form of Auntie Grace's video to show me the error of my ways.

Make the diagnosis, then find the cure. Sounds simple. But what can a man do when he has always played totally naturally, never received much tuition, and suddenly finds his game literally falling apart?

I knew I had to get my head straight. That was of paramount importance. Get that right, and the rest would probably fall into place. So I took a decision which, without question, has produced more improvement in my batting than any other single factor throughout my career. I altered my stance from the orthodox, with bat tapping on the ground, to the unconventional upright, bat held in the air. It took a little time to adapt, and some trial and error to make it feel natural. But, when I had played that way for only a short time, I knew beyond doubt that I would never change back again.

When the 1984 season ended I was given various awards as 'batsman of the year' for scoring around 2,500 runs in county cricket, far and away my best-ever year. But whenever people posed the obvious question about what I had done to improve my game, my answer was always the same. In 1984 I physically did nothing different from 1983. Mentally, perhaps, I was more mature. As a batsman I was certainly more experienced. But the major change in my game dated back to spring 1979 when I took the plunge with my new stance.

People laughed at first. I was not the first to stand with his bat off the ground, as Tony Greig had been doing it some years earlier, but I had certainly exaggerated the position, holding my bat higher than anyone else and making very definite corrective movements to ensure my head was absolutely straight before each ball.

I remember when I went to South Africa for the SAB tour. I was only a name, and maybe a face, to the cricket-watching public out there. They had never seen me bat, unless they had chanced to attend a Green Point club game six winters earlier, and the sight of me shaping up with my bat raised behind me and my head twisting to look down my shoulder blade drew many an incredulous comment, mostly to the effect that they must be seeing the wrong Gooch. They could not believe that I was the batsman who had taken three Test centuries off West Indies not too many months earlier, and probably suspected I was a ringer. The reaction quickly changed when I began to make some runs, however, and, by the time I went back to Cape Town the next winter to play for Western Province, it was my turn to look incredulous at the number of boys, teenage and even younger, who were using the upright stance in their park knockabouts.

It has become my trademark and I am proud of it, because it was never introduced to my game as any sort of gimmick, but an essential measure which has produced exactly the desired results.

I am well aware that there are those who consider it ugly, others who feel it is more than faintly ridiculous, but I am always prepared to defend it against all criticism and have the figures to back me up. A lot of players are now using the stance in county cricket, though few with the bat raised as high as me, and I think the initial suspicion has gone and people have come to realize that it is, in fact, the most natural way to bat.

Coaches will always work furiously to instil in players the need to bring the bat back straight and bring it down straight. In the upright stance, the bat is already almost at the top of its arc and it is very nearly impossible to bring it down across the line of the ball. As the bowler delivers, I bring my bat down a few inches and then back up again, but this is a semi-conscious addition to the method. The main thing is that I am properly lined up, sideways on and with my head perfectly straight. I always had the ability to hit the ball cleanly but there were technical flaws in my game which this change has played an enormous part in smoothing out. In the mid-1970s, when I was first picked for England, I made runs at county level and was considered a highly promising player. But when I look back now on that period I can see I was very rough-edged.

My game has always been based on attack. I go to meet the ball rather than allowing it to come onto the bat as, for instance, Keith Fletcher does so successfully. Where 'Fletch' would be playing the ball late, working it into the gaps in the field, I want to be at the ball and striking it in front of the wicket. This is all very well, and can make for exciting viewing, but the basics of batting are just as important whether you are a disciple of Fletcher or Gooch. If you start to play across your front leg, as I was doing on that fateful Australian tour, you will find plenty of ways to get out. I still do it occasionally, but the new stance, coupled with a higher level of concentration which I can now apply to my game, means that I am technically a much more correct player than ever I used to be.

The knowledge that I am doing everything the right way has added unknown confidence to my game. I have never been scared of fast bowling, but I am now at the point where I would feel happier facing Joel Garner on a quick wicket than one of the medium-pace trundlers on green-tops which confront us too often in county cricket.

I only once had the chance to face Garner in 1984. While the West Indian quick bowlers were causing widespread misery around England on their way to achieving a 5–0 whitewash in the Test series, I came no closer to them than the television, except for the one game in June when the all-conquering tourists came to Chelmsford to meet Essex. I had the immense personal satisfaction of becoming the first man to take a century off the West Indians during their tour. Gratifying though it was to hear the cries go up that I would make a big difference to the Test series and must at once have my ban rescinded, I took no great notice of either statement. I knew there was absolutely no chance of the TCCB climbing down at this late stage and waving me back into Test cricket on good-behaviour remission. And, even if they had, I was under no illusions about the size of the task facing anyone against this formidable West Indies machine. I might have scored a hundred against them in between their more major engagements, but it was a very different matter expecting me to have any material influence on such a one-sided Test series.

So I contented myself with helping Essex achieve a unique double and, come September, I could really have asked for nothing more. Not only did we retain the championship, we also won the John Player League for a second time. Several counties have won two competitions in a season before, including ourselves, but it was commonly agreed that this was the toughest 'double' of them all, as both require consistency over four-and-a-half months yet each demands its own disciplines and tactics. To master both, very different forms of cricket and emerge on top in a single season was an achivement which will not easily be repeated.

Sunday cricket, with its large, enthusiastic crowds and its extensive TV coverage, carries an element of glamour which the three-day game, often played before empty grounds and largely ignored by the popular media, can no longer command. But this does not alter the fact that the Championship is the most highly-prized of all the honours available to a county team. If we at Essex had to choose a competition to win each year, we would not hesitate in nominating the Championship, as it holds all our attentions for so much of the season and is accepted, at least among cricketers and true cricket followers, as the ultimate test of a team. So it was in 1984. The knowledge that we had won it the previous year changed nothing; our determination was just as strong to prove all over again that we were the best team in England and, despite a sustained challenge by Notts which came desperately close to frustrating us, that is exactly what we did.

None of us will forget the evening of Tuesday, 11 September. It was the final day of the season: we had beaten Lancashire inside two days at Old Trafford and it was all now in the hands of Notts. If they were to win against Somerset at Taunton, they would hang on to the narrow lead they had taken into this last round of matches and become champions again. If they drew or lost, we kept the title. We had all been summoned to Chelmsford for a 6 p.m. reception thrown by Britannic, the new championship sponsors. Whatever the outcome at Taunton, the reception would go on; only its mood was liable to change.

As fate had it, the game in Somerset was coming to its agonizing climax as I drove to the ground. I had Radio Two on in the car, and, as I turned into the car park at Chelmsford, they went over live to Henry Blofeld on the ground. Like everyone else in our side, I had been following the scores all day and it seemed that the game was slipping away from Notts. Ian Botham, having dictated terms throughout, had made a good declaration, challenging Notts to go for the target, as they had to, but retaining the upper hand. When one or two early wickets fell it seemed they had no chance, but Clive Rice is an inspiring captain when the moment comes to lead by example and he did so now, playing an innings which changed the course of the game. He was out in the nick of time, from our point of view, but, as 'Blowers' took up the commentary in his very excited Old Etonian tones, a new danger had presented itself to our peace of mind in the ample shape of Mike Bore, the Yorkshire-born medium-pace bowler who was making a belated comeback to first-team cricket at the age of 37. Botham kept his spinners, Marks and Booth, working in tandem, and Bore kept hitting them for four.

Keith Fletcher and his wife, Sue, were sitting in their car outside the pavilion. The rest of the side was already gathered upstairs, a radio on. I went over and suggested 'Fletch' came up to join us, but he wouldn't. He even sent Sue out of the car, so that he could be alone with his thoughts. I knew how much this meant to him and left him to it.

Notts were one six-hit short of victory when Bore slightly under-struck a drive against Booth, the young left-armer, and was caught on the boundary. The roar that went up inside our pavilion could probably have been heard all around the town and, when the captain finally did join us, there was the customary champagne celebration, interrupted by callers from radio, TV, newspapers and general well-wishers. It was a great and memorable evening, but I know I spared a thought more than once for how the Notts boys must have been feeling. So near and yet so far.

Clever punters, who had backed Notts at 33–1 ante-post with

one especially generous bookmaker, possibly begrudged us our bubbly. But I think a long and logical look at events will show that we kept going just that little bit better than our rivals when the heat was on. It will also show that Gooch made runs, Lever again took wickets. It will not show the day when we took the contest by the scruff of the neck, won a match that had seemed beyond us and perhaps turned the tide in our favour.

We were playing Middlesex at Lord's in the second week of August, a Middlesex side still nurturing their own hopes of the title and plainly among the toughest of opponents on their own ground. The shame of it was that England was playing the West Indies in the Fifth Test, over the river at the Oval, but if this shifted public attention away from our game it took nothing away from the quality of the cricket.

There was a panic on the first morning when our kit van, which we had entrusted to the two junior members of the side, Chris Gladwin and Paul Prichard, squealed through the Grace Gates with only minutes to spare before the game began. But thereafter we settled into three days of gripping cricket – probably as good a Championship match as I have taken part in for years. A little feeling between the teams is always evident when we play Middlesex – not in any unpleasant or overtly aggressive way, but just because a good deal of pride and prestige is always at stake. This time, with both sides virtually at full strength and certainly at full stretch for honours, the atmosphere was tense and expectant.

For two days, we just held the initiative, but Middlesex, having trailed on first innings and found themselves in a position from which victory was impossible, set themselves to deny us the win and looked like succeeding. By tea on the last day they had crept into a lead of around 200, with two wickets left and a maximum of 40 overs remaining. We sat subdued in the dressing-room, and when I looked across at 'Fletch' he shook his head, indicating that he now thought the task was beyond us. Logic pointed to him being right, but within a few minutes of the resumption we had taken the last couple of wickets and hope surged again.

The target was 211 in 33 overs. Under normal circumstances it might not even have been attempted, and there were those in our side who thought it pointless to try now. But my viewpoint was this: Championships can be won and lost on one brave decision and seldom, if ever, are they won by a team declining to take the odd risk. I was firmly of the opinion that we should go for the runs and confident that if we did find ourselves in trouble we still had the depth of batting necessary to play out time.

I was, of course, in a position to take things into my own hands, and when Norman Cowans bowled two or three loose overs with the new-ball we had 30 on the board almost before Middlesex had realized what was happening. There was then no turning back. We lost wickets at intervals, but everyone played their part in the chase. The glory fell on me, for a century which gave me tremendous pleasure, but, after all the doubts over whether the target was even feasible, the victory was essentially a team effort and one which gave us a great psychological boost for the run-in towards the title.

Most people will expect me to name that Lord's century as my best innings of an unforgettable summer, but I would not agree. My own choice would be a hundred I made in a lost cause, during our home defeat by Notts in May. What pleased me so much about this innings was that it required concentration over a long period, and that is something which has so often been my downfall in the past. I have said before that I felt expectations of 2,000 runs in a season from me were false because I have never been a consistent, long-innings player. The 1984 season, I am pleased to say, began to correct this inadequacy in my game, and the hundred against Notts set the tone and gave me the confidence to go on.

There was a very good reason why the 1984 season gave everyone at the Essex club a smug sense of satisfaction. Not only did we win honours, but we did it with a transitional side. Against the expectations of, it seems, most people outside the county, we had emerged from the successful but static decade of a settled side and brought in new, young players. To do so was necessary. To do so while retaining both the spirit and success of the side was admirable.

Foster and Pringle were the first to be fitted into the jigsaw, along with David East, when Neil Smith, our long-serving wicketkeeper, retired. In 1983 we brought in Chris Gladwin to open the batting with me, and in 1984 Paul Prichard earned, and then held down, a batting place. I heard some supporters around the ground speaking of Gladwin as a prospective England player during 1984. I even read his name being proposed as a candidate for the tour of India. This was premature as the end of the season arrived and Chris had still not scored a Championship hundred. He had, it is true, made one against Cambridge University and three times been out in the nineties against counties, giving his wicket away with a mix of recklessness and nervousness each time. But to talk of him in Test terms showed a desperation brought on by England's continuing struggles.

This is not intended to run down Chris. He is an exciting, aggressive young player and one in whom I have had a personal interest since I played club cricket in the same East Ham Corinthians side as his father, Ron. I was 15 at the time and Chris can have been no more than six, but I used to throw a tennis ball to him and he would whack it around. It may sound ridiculous, but even at that age it is possible to tell whether someone has a natural feel for a cricket bat. Chris always had that.

It did not take him long to fit neatly into the dressing-room humour. Chris is a typical East Ender, a flat-hatted barrow-boy at heart. He has a gruff voice, ready wit and, when he came into the side, he called everyone 'Guv'. So that, naturally enough, became his nickname, and it suits him well.

Prichard is a contrast, both as player and person. Quiet to the point of being shy, a great rarity in our side, he is technically better and more solid than 'Guv' and, if he sometimes looks one-paced at this early stage of his career, experience will give him the know-how and the confidence to accelerate when the time is right. He has been coveted like a future treasure by Essex, brought gradually into the Championship side at number six or seven and promoted to open in our final match of last season, where he made a fine hundred at Old Trafford when Gladwin was left out.

Sensibly and deliberately, Prichard has been confined to three-day cricket for the senior side and spared the confusion that many young batsmen feel in having to adapt rapidly from trying to play long innings in the Championship to batting with almost sacrificial aggression in the limited-overs competitions. We are fortunate to have the resources to leave him out. It is a luxury many clubs could not afford. But I am convinced it is the correct way of introducing a young batsman and that we would have many more technically accomplished players now emerging to challenge for Test places if counties had not been willing, or obliged, to make the fundamental error of bringing them immediately into the hectic cricket of the John Player League.

In years to come, Prichard will undoubtedly come into the one-day team but hopefully, the careful grooming process will have prepared him well. His main job, I fancy, will be to take over the middle-order position held for so long with such distinction by 'Fletch', when the captain finally decides to hang up his boots.

While the youngsters all played a creditable part in the Championship triumph, however, it was 'old man' Lever who really stole the show again. With bowlers like Pringle and Foster around, it might have been expected that 'J.K.' would begin to fade into the background. Not a bit of it. For the fourth time in six years he took more than 100 first-class wickets, this time despite playing the last few weeks of the season on only one effective leg.

Pound for pound, match for match, I believe John is the best bowler in England. Richard Hadlee has no peer as the most effective cricketer in the Championship but John's strength, consistency and unrivalled enthusiasm have, over the years, won more county games than any other bowler in the country. His bowling is built on physical stamina; he is actually happiest when he has the ball in his hands and there can even be a tendency for us to bowl him too much, both for his own good and occasionally for the good of the side. Far better this risk, however, than the failing of so many lesser bowlers who give the impression that they never really enjoy or relish their job and are quite content to come off after five overs and skulk at fine leg for the rest of a session.

John's greatest value to the team has frequently been his ability to keep going for hours at a time, closing down one end while the other bowlers rotate. He took 67 wickets for England in 20 Tests before being banned, but I believe the main reason he was not a greater success is that he seldom bowled for long enough. Mike Brearley would often take him off after five or six overs, plainly disappointed, but John has always been accustomed to long spells in which he improves as he settles into a rhythm. He has never been a shock bowler, never had the pace to be, but I think he might well have taken many more wickets for England if he had been handled differently.

Despite another phenomenally successful season, John remained sceptical about his chances of being considered for further England caps when his ban ended but there was no doubt in my mind that, if fit enough, he deserves to be among the leading candidates. It was a mystery to me why he never appeared to be especially popular with the England selectors, but he still won most of his caps when the competition for fast bowling places was very much fiercer than it is now. In the late 1970s, Willis, Old, Botham, Hendrick and Lever were all at their bowling peaks and they could obviously not all play in the same side. John was very often the unlucky one. Now, however, the others are all either retired or well past their best, and only John remains to challenge the new breed, led by Foster and Cowans. There is a sizeable generation gap – John can give them both more than a dozen years – but the fact that he is 36 should not, I believe, have any detrimental effect on his chances. It is difficult to name any young, top-class seam and swing bowlers outside the ranks of those who have already played Test cricket, so it is not as if John would be keeping out a younger man of equal ability. His record shows that he can still bowl the same quota of overs as he has always done and, if the knee which troubled him in 1984, and on which he needed an autumn operation, stands up to full-time cricket again, I see no reason why the man who may well be the most popular of all county cricketers among the players themselves should not add a few more honours to his collection before he eventually stops playing.

We did not win the Sunday League simply by an extension of the style and tactics which won us the Championship. John Player League games were approached with an entirely different game-plan and, in many cases, a very different cast list. Tactics obviously vary a little from match to match but our Sunday strategy was well-oiled and well conceived. It stood the test of time and, from some distance out, I was in no real doubt that we were the best side in England at the 40-overs game. To some counties, the league is an imposition, something to be endured, not real cricket. While I can sympathise to some extent, I can't share the view. Maybe because we have usually done well in the competition, the Essex players enjoy the atmosphere and the challenge of the John Player League. It may not be cricket in its accepted first-class form, but it is popular with the public, and no professional can afford to knock that.

One of the men who did not play in our Sunday side was Neil Foster. This probably surprised people, Neil being an England bowler, but the fact is he had not acquired the experience to bowl off 15 yards and was proving expensive. Bowling on Sundays is a specialist art and you cannot afford to carry someone who is finding things hard, so for Neil's sake and our own he was generally left out, along with Paul Prichard, and the experienced and reliable allrounders Turner and Phillip were drafted in.

A side-effect of the very healthy competition for places that has been bred at our club in recent seasons was that someone was likely to be put out. Keith Pont hardly played in the first-team at all in 1984, despite finishing third in our batting averages the previous season; we missed him for his manic humour and his bubbling company, but he took the demotion well. Stuart Turner, who had been gradually edged out of the Championship side by the development of Pringle, found it harder to accept. He had been a regular for 15 years, never quite reaching the heights of achievement needed to win him England consideration but never, never giving less than his best. His record of almost 10,000 runs and 800 wickets speaks for itself – but time marches on. Stuart passed his fortieth birthday during the 1983 season and, willing though he was to battle on, 'Fletch' took the view that he was now better suited to specialising in the one-day competitions, where his tight seam bowling and low-order hitting is invaluable.

In a sense it is a blessing that Stuart and 'Nobby' are the age they are. If they were ten years younger and we found ourselves similarly placed, we would be hard put to hold onto them. As it is, I think they have come to look forward to Sundays, when their parts are crucial to success. 'Nobby' is ideally suited to Sunday cricket; he is a potential match-winner, an instant hero and an occasional flop.

With the steady Turner the ideal foil, both our bowling and our middle-order batting are strong in depth.

Pringle is another key man on Sundays. He now bats at number four, where his underrated clean hitting can rapidly accelerate the progress, and he is entrusted with the vital job of bowling at 'the death' when, if the game is anything like evenly poised, he will have to contend with shots being played against every ball, and need a steady nerve as well as a consistent length and line.

I see my job on Sundays as being the anchor man, not in the sense that I will plod through the innings without an aggressive thought in my head, but that I should at least try to be there at the end. By the very nature of my game I will look to score very fast once I get through the first half of the innings, and if I am there for the full 40 overs we are guaranteed an imposing score. Of course, it doesn't often happen.

Chris Gladwin and I worked hard on our running, an area in which we were not at all proficient early on. For the 40-overs game, a good understanding is vital, as stolen singles and twos turned into threes can make a critical difference to the total, and possible result, at the end of the day. We watched other sides taking ones everywhere and knew that we had some ground to make up, but by the end of the season we had improved beyond recognition and I had come to the conclusion that, with a willing partner, you will both make your ground nine times out of ten on the dodgiest-looking runs.

The revelation of the Sunday season was the old boy himself. 'Fletch' got annoyed one day when we mischievously suggested he should drop down the order in the league as he was unable to slog. He suddenly began to produce a shot that none of us had seen him play before, quite a feat after all these years. He would adopt an even more crouched stance than usual – it became known as the 'Mad Marty' position in the dressing-room – and club everything over mid-wicket with a short-arm pull stroke. Despite his advancing years, Keith still has one of the best eyes in the game and, when he set himself to play in this fashion, he was not easy to bowl at. The pitch had to be quick enough to support it, of course, but the faster the bowling the farther it disappeared. He took on, and visibly riled, several international quick bowlers and Winston Davis,

Glamorgan's West Indian, was almost beside himself when he received the full brunt of the Fletcher treatment.

Success really does breed success and it often seemed we could do nothing wrong on Sundays. Winning becomes a good habit, confidence swells to such a degree that players go out with hardly a thought of defeat, and it can make a great difference to a side in the high-pressure confines of a 40-overs game. There was no better example of this syndrome than our match against Hampshire during the festival week at Castle Park in Colchester. We had made 250, which is enough to win most Sunday games, but runs are seldom in short supply on this pleasant ground and Hampshire looked to be winning it hands down. With three overs left they still needed 18 runs, but they had eight wickets in hand. Suddenly they panicked, two key men were run out and they lost their way. The points were ours.

It was this way many a time, it seemed, during the long, sunny summer of 1984. We lost the odd game, both on Sundays and in the Championship. We did not reach Lord's for one of the cup finals. But we will not remember the year for these minor irritations, much more as surely the greatest season in the club's history, the year when we proved we have a big future as well as a recent past to be proud of.

11
England in eclipse

In November of last year, England's cricketers came under the microscope as never before. Defeat in the Bombay Test, the first of a new series against India, created an unwanted record of 12 successive Tests without victory. Lord's felt obliged to act. A working party was set up, comprising nine experts under the chairmanship of Charles Palmer, who is also chairman of the Test and County Cricket Board. Their brief was wide but their aims unmistakeable – discover the reasons for the failure of the England Test team.

The proverbial needle in the haystack was possibly easier to locate, but not by much. There are no simple remedies to the situation in which English cricket found itself. No one change, nor even two or three, can dramatically arrest the decline and return the barometer to 'fair'.

It would be the easiest thing in the world for me to boast that things would never have reached this state if the board had not banned 15 of their best players for three years. There would even be a certain amount of truth in it. But it is by no means the full answer to the equation. That England would have been stronger with all the players available is surely undeniable; they may even have won a few more matches to alleviate the immediate need for board enquiries. But this would not have changed everything.

Let me make it clear I am not one of those who delight in knocking the English game. I happen to believe that the system we play under is generally popular and enjoyable, and that the enthusiasm for cricket in our country is as great now as it is anywhere in the world. There is also much to be admired about the set-up of our cricket – it is administered much more professionally here than elsewhere, our umpires leave their overseas colleagues far behind and our facilities have improved a good deal during my career. But, as in any other sport, when the national team is playing poorly, post-mortems are the order of the day. If the England football team went 12 matches without a win, the manager would probably be sacked. Cricket, thank goodness, is not quite so callous but, with the ever-increasing media pressures promoting the importance of winning above all else, we are some way down that road.

England's performances over recent years do not make happy reading. Until the India series, it had been six years since we won overseas, a travel sickness which seems to be afflicting every country with the perennial exception of West Indies. And even at home where, apart from the 5–0 hammering by Clive Lloyd's men, results have been appreciably better, there has been the odd slump – the terribly undistinguished performance against Sri Lanka, the Test newcomers, in 1984 particularly sticks in the throat in this respect.

Bob Willis can at least claim series wins over India, Pakistan and New Zealand when the side was under his captaincy. David Gower, until his change of fortune in India, had not even won a Test – in fact his record as skipper was a maudlin three draws and seven defeats. I felt sorry for him. It was not all his fault, by a very long way.

One of the greatest handicaps England sides have laboured under in recent years has been a shortage of high-quality seam bowlers. Until recently, I would have said simply fast bowlers, but now that is no longer the case. Since the suspension of Chris Old, John Lever and Mike Hendrick robbed England of the three best bowlers in the category, no seamer of comparable class has emerged to claim his England place. For this to happen is a stern and unexpected indictment because, throughout the 1970s, the great strength of English cricket was in seam bowling; now that one generation has, for various reasons, passed on, there are no heirs apparent.

The lack of genuine quick bowling is not such a surprise. One has only to look back through the career of Bob Willis to appreciate that this is nothing new. Bob played only a few Tests in partnership with John Snow, his predecessor and to some degree his hero. That apart, he has scarcely ever had a partner with the new-ball of a speed even similar to his own. Australia have had Lillee and Thomson, then Lawson and Hogg. West Indies have had an endless conveyor belt of pacemen. We have had only one in more than a decade who has properly made the grade.

Others have flattered, the most persistent and probably the most unlucky of these being Graham Dilley. There were times, especially in West Indies in 1981, when 'Picca', as Bob Willis wittily nicknamed him, looked a genuine prospect. He had a fine action, the touches of hostility which every fast bowler needs, and authentic pace to match most bowlers operating at that time in the world. He impressed and shook up some pretty good judges, Clive Lloyd among them, but to my way of thinking he also let himself down in some foolish instances. In one game, I remember, he ripped off the sole of his boot through the drag in his delivery stride. Fair enough – no one would crucify him for that. But Graham had brought only one other pair of bowling boots out to the Caribbean – something which amazed Bob Willis – and had managed to leave those back at the hotel. This was not just careless but unprofessional.

Graham, however, was only young. If his temperament was not quite what it needed to be and his mind was not wholly organized on the job in hand, he at least had the excuse of immaturity. And he did have talent in plenty. It was a tragedy for English cricket when he suffered the latest in a series of injuries while in Pakistan in the spring of 1984, a nerve condition which put him out of the game for at least 12 months. Kent, his county, report encouraging progress, but only time will tell if he can recapture the speed which gave him such promise.

With Graham injured and Bob now at last retired, the England opening attack is more flexible, but less formidable, than it has been since I began playing the game. Norman Cowans had graduated swiftly from county newcomer to number one strike bowler in the Test side. Too quickly. He can bowl fast, of that there is no question. But at the highest level there is far more to the job than that. He was hurried into Test cricket due to a shortage of alternatives and life has been made hard for him, no matter how fortunate he may initially consider himself. I heard good reports coming back from India last winter of the improvement in his line and control, which was pleasing. But there is a long ladder to climb before Cowans can be put alongside Willis, Snow and the bowling spearheads of the past.

Neil Foster is probably our brightest prospect, and not just because he plays for my own county. Neil has once or twice been questioned over his general attitude – I thought it very wrong that he should come back from his first England tour with ideas above his station. But again, one can blame immaturity for that. Neil, to his credit, settled back into a county routine and, in the summer of 1984, took more than 80 first-class wickets, which was a very fine performance. In the long term, he could be a great asset to England, as his action is good, his control excellent. Like Cowans, he was chosen at a time when he had barely established himself in county cricket and the selectors were vainly scouring the country for a sign of seam bowlers with class and experience.

I have no miracle cure for the shortage. Nobody has. Everyone has their own theories, their own pet remedies. But it is just like the common cold – different people will treat it in different ways and some will be convinced that their method works. But the only sure cure is time. I have no doubt that the wheel of fortune will turn and that before too long some hefty, muscular quick bowlers will burst upon the county scene with 'Test future' written all over their chests. Fast bowlers, more than any other category of cricketers, really are born and not made and, much as I admire the efforts made by people like Ted Dexter and Willis to create the mould of the pace bowler in young men who, in many cases, had never played cricket in their lives, I have grave reservations about their chances of success.

There are a number of popular, specific reasons quoted for the fast bowler famine. One-day cricket is the most frequently heard, and there are plenty of grounds to justify this belief. Sunday cricket, bowling off limited run-ups to defensive fields, is potentially designed to take the edge off fast bowlers, who then have to readjust and rush in off their full runs again the following morning.

It seems more likely, however, that the proliferation of one-day games has a detrimental effect on young batsmen than on bowlers. The batsmen coming into the professional game are forced to make wholesale adjustments in their technique and their approach from one day to the next. They may be bowled two balls exactly the same, one on a Sunday and the other on a Monday, but they will be expected to try to hit one for four and block or leave the other. The textbook is compromised on a Sunday and every batsman has to forget most of the good lessons he has learned and pick up runs in whatever way possible. This can be hard enough for an experienced player, let alone for someone just trying to make his mark in a side.

Sub-standard pitches is another favourite theory trotted out to explain all ills. I would take notice here of the players who have been around 15 or 20 years and can speak of the time before I began playing, but I can only say that in my experience the majority of county pitches are just as good, or bad, as they were a decade ago. I have never played on consistently quick wickets and I have not played on many where one can be confident of an even bounce.

This is not to say that an overall improvement in pitch conditions would not be of great help. If a batsman knows he can expect the ball to come on at regular pace and height, he will be encouraged to play technically better and with more confidence which, in turn, will assist him when he does not on an occasional poor wicket. And, if the pace of English pitches was generally sharper, more youngsters would be encouraged to run in and bowl fast because they would be able to see the evidence of their efforts. As it is, far too many grow tired of the fruitless slog and revert to bowling medium-pace trundlers.

If I had to point to one single area in which English cricket has lost its way, however, it would be the facilities available in schools. Having now travelled to most of the world's cricket-playing countries and seen their schooling systems at first hand, it has been brought home to me just how far we lag behind. Money cannot alone be the drawback, as sponsors seem to be readily found for most other areas of cricket. I know there are people at Lord's, within the National Cricket Association set-up, who work long and tirelessly in this direction, trying to improve facilities for young, potential cricketers. But it seems we are not making any great progress. Clubs around the country are exempt from the blame as, in general, they seem very much more alert to the possibilities of training cricketers at a young age, and I know many clubs whose colts coaching schemes go down to eight- and nine-year-olds. It is the schools who seem to be at fault.

I can appreciate that the restraints, chiefly financial, within the teaching profession do not allow for the appointment of a full-time cricket coach at any but the most sports-minded of private schools. And if there is no cricket coach, then who takes the boys for cricket? Sometimes, a school is lucky enough to have on its staff one, or even two, club cricketers of reasonable standard and enough enthusiasm for the game to devote some of their spare time to supervising net sessions, taking the school teams away for games and generally organizing them. But most schools are not in that fortunate position and if cricket is played at all it will be taken by a maths master, on a period off with no aptitude for the game and even less enthusiasm. The boys, naturally enough, grow disenchanted with cricket and turn to something that the school finds it less of a problem to organize, like football, rugby or athletics. Cricket coaching needs specialist knowledge, individual tuition. That is why so few schools play it to any level these days. It is also why the flow of schoolboy cricketers into the first-class game has slowed from a rush to a trickle.

You need to be dedicated or lucky to do it the other way. Those who get into club cricket at a young age are going to be well looked after. Those whose parents are keen on cricket will probably be shepherded in the right direction. And a few will simply have so much natural ability that someone will pretty soon notice them. Ian Botham was doubtless one of this latter group. So far as I am aware he did not have much opportunity to play cricket at school, but that was never going to stop him. Sadly, there are very few like him around.

Botham's absence from the England party to tour India last winter gave it an inevitably unbalanced look. For six years now, he has been the man to whom England have looked for inspiration. If he didn't do it with the bat, the feeling was that he would produce a miracle with the ball or, at the very least, hold a stunning catch or two. Batting at number six or seven and bowling among the front-line seamers, he was the ultimate allrounder and England have rapidly realized that it basically needs two players of ordinary ability to replace him.

I don't at all blame Ian for deciding to take a break from Test cricket. In fact, I think he was well advised to do so. Thinking back to the way I have sometimes felt, especially on tour of if things have been going wrong, I know all too well how constant international cricket can leave its mark on the most resilient of characters, leaving a jaded and uninspired feeling in which, physically and mentally, you are unable to give of your best. Perhaps what I am saying is that there is now too much international cricket. It is certainly shortening playing lives and it might just be dissipating the interest of the public. But that is another subject.

It was impossible for Ian to maintain his remarkable standards when he was being asked to do so much. Personally, I think it was wrong to use him as a stock bowler in Test cricket. His great value was as an attacking bowler, doing the unexpected, occasionally conceding needless boundaries but then, a moment later, taking a wicket. And then another. England were at their best when Willis and Botham were allowed to operate as the strike men and someone such as Mike Hendrick employed to block up an end with his nagging, economical length-and-line bowling. Despite that, Ian has already broken many records in his astonishing England career and he is likely to overtake Bob Willis, and probably Dennis Lillee, as the leading wicket-taker in Test cricket history. It will be a fitting testimony, and quite extraordinary for someone who also spends as much time batting as Ian has done, and if he does improve on Lillee's figure I think the record will stand for a very long while, certainly for the conceivable future under the current set-up of international cricket.

I am sure Ian suffers from motivation problems. I do, too, but for him – with so much already achieved – the problem of finding new goals must be doubly difficult. He still turns on the full volume of his talents when something, or somebody, has activated him with a fresh incentive, but he cannot do it day after day as once he could. This, I suspect, was another reason for taking a winter off. He wanted to recharge his batteries and come back feeling fresh and positive for the visit of Australia. Admirable sentiments, of course because, to virtually every English cricketer, the series against Australia is still the most important series of all, no matter their current strength in relation to West Indies.

Maybe, though, there was one more reason why Ian thought it prudent to do what does not to him come naturally and shrink away out of the limelight for a while.

He has become the hottest property in world cricket. I say that without any hesitation at all as, despite the phenomenal success of West Indies, they have no one with the charisma, or the allround talent, to match Botham at his best. So, as number one, he attracts all kinds of extraneous pressures, the type of pressures which have destroyed many superbly talented men in other sporting fields, men like George Best and John Conteh, who eventually appeared far more in the gossip columns than the sports pages.

Ian lives the life to complement his image. He would probably not fit the bill as the schoolboy's vision of the dedicated superstar – he dislikes going to bed early, plays practical jokes and sometimes needs the crudest type of verbal motivation to bring out the brilliant best in him. Inevitably, he has attracted the wrong kind of publicity and been subjected to various different slurs on his lifestyle.

The worst, from cricket's standpoint, was the allegations that he was involved in drugs parties during England's tour of New Zealand in early 1984. This was the sort of scandal that the game and all its individuals shy away from. I was not on the tour in question. I have no idea what did or did not happen and no wish to get involved. But it does seem to me to be just possible that, this last winter, Ian wanted a break from the almost intolerable gaze of the media on his every move.

Botham at his best is great company on tour, whether you are trying to avoid his dressing-room pranks or just talking music and football with him of an evening. I am sure that the more experienced England players missed him for this in India last winter, almost as much as they undoubtedly missed him on the field. But I do feel it might have done England, and certain players, a bit of good to be without him for a while. In playing terms they had to learn to live without him and adapt to the gaping hole he left. In social terms, the dominant role that he took upon himself would have disappeared. Ian, by his nature, has to lead. He called the tune among the players, on and off the field, and it will have been no bad thing for them to find a little more independence during his, hopefully brief, absence.

Cricket, I think, just fits into the hectic life style Ian enjoys. It is his job, occasionally it fires his imagination, often he is outstandingly good at it. But there are so many other things he wants to do that I wonder how long the game can hold him. He is now 29 and could theoretically play on for another six or seven years at the highest level. I hope he does, as he can make so much difference to our team. Bob Willis once said that when Botham is playing well, England are playing well, and there was a lot of sense in that remark. He is still far and away the best cricketer we have got – in fact in terms of pure ability he is also the best individual batsman we have got – and I hope someone emerges who can psyche him up and continue to produce the goods from him as Mike Brearley was so adept at doing.

Even Ian could do nothing to check the flow of defeats against West Indies last summer, but he could certainly never have been accused of showing he was intimidated by the bowling. This was an issue which arose time and again, as I suppose it always will when one team has such a strong hand in fast bowling and the other does not.

Watching on television, as I was, it was not easy to come to any firm conclusions about the amount of short-pitched bowling but on at least one occasion I did feel that Malcolm Marshall, their most effective bowler, was allowed to bowl too many bouncers. Four short balls an over must constitute an attempt to intimidate because, if the batsman has shown he is unwilling to hook, as most of England's did, there is no way the ball can get a wicket other than through an involuntary and unlucky attempt at self-defence.

The umpiring has to be questioned here. Legislation on intimidation does seem to be very cloudy but it is surely in the hands of the umpires to be firm in their interpretation. The West Indians would not agree to the rule of one bouncer per over in any case, but it is a woolly rule which can easily be challenged – four balls an over can go through at chest, rib or throat height and be allowed by an umpire, despite being potentially far more dangerous than four balls sailing over the batsman's head.

Talk of painting a white line across the pitch is nothing more than a camouflage for weak officiating. Umpires have the authority to take a bowler off for the remainder of an innings and I feel it should have been used more often than it has.

I have no doubt some of the England batsmen were unsettled by playing cricket against such unremittingly hostile bowling but at that level of cricket I don't think they can have many complaints. If you cannot get behind the ball and follow the basic principles, you should not be playing Test cricket.

Never in my life have I been physically scared by short-pitched bowling. Just once, however, I was both confused and apprehensive. It was in 1980, during the low-scoring Trent Bridge Test against West Indies which, eventually, we lost only narrowly. Michael Holding was bowling very fast and for some reason I just didn't feel right. My feet were not moving as quickly or as accurately as they should have been and it was in my mind that he could hit me if I did not sharpen up.

If I went out to start an innings thinking about being hit, however, I could not play the game. I would not be thinking of the right things, I would not be doing the natural things when I should be, and consequently my entire technique would collapse. I have known this happen to players – it apparently happened to more than one when England toured Australia in 1974–75 and it has certainly been a problem more recently against West Indies. Guts and courage are as important as technical ability in such a situation, which explains why Peter Willey was so very effective against the West Indians. No one could ever intimidate him!

I had high hopes that Derek Randall might play an important part against Marshall, Garner and company in 1984, not because he is anything remotely similar to Willey in temperament – he is not – but because he has the ability to play shots which can be a great distraction to a quick bowler. I recall Derek doing just this when he opened the batting against Pakistan in 1982. Imran was bowling very fast, but Derek made a hundred, admittedly through the unconventional and improvised, but a hundred of sheer frustration for Pakistan and their captain, nonetheless. Last year, however, I felt he looked vulnerable against the fast men.

My sympathy might have been muted for the top-order England batsmen, but I felt very sorry for the tailenders. Against most other sides, you can be optimistic about your last few batsmen picking up fifty or sixty runs, but not against West Indies. If a number ten or eleven batsman blocks half a dozen deliveries with any degree of certainty, he is odds-on to get a bouncer whistling past his nose. Most will then freeze with terror, because they are simply not equipped to deal with it. If that is not intimidation, I don't know what is.

The other topic on which West Indies brought heated discussion was over-rates. They were undoubtedly the main culprits in the downward trend of overs bowled, but it is very hard to argue the point with them. They will say that if they bowl 20 overs an hour, Test matches will be all over inside three days. On recent evidence they would be right.

Only half-a-dozen years ago Test matches managed an average of 500 overs yet last year that figure had dropped to 388, not substantially greater than the number bowled in a three-day County Championship game. I find it hard to work out how sides with more than two quick bowlers, operating off long runs, ever got through 21 or 22 overs in an hour, as we are told they did, but while I remain sceptical about the size of the problem (I don't, for instance, believe that it is a burning issue with the cricket-watching public) I do think 16 overs an hour should be the minimum acceptable level. Last year at Essex we fell just below that figure, and if we repeat it in 1985 when the new Test and County Cricket Board fining system comes into operation, we will be liable for £14,000 – a sobering thought.

My mind strayed frequently to Test cricket during the winter of 1984–85. It was a winter in England, a rare luxury; a chance to train with West Ham, to go and watch them play on Saturdays, spend as much time as I wanted with Brenda and my young daughter, Hannah, a chance to spend Christmas at home and see snow on the ground. Little things, but they mean a lot when you have been overseas for so many winters. I listened to the radio commentaries crackling down the line from Bombay, Delhi, Calcutta and the rest, all places I had been to three years earlier, just prior to the most momentous decision of my career.

I could not help wondering whether I really would be forgiven. It mattered not that *I* thought there was little to be forgiven – others plainly thought differently. I wondered whether, the lifting of the ban in April 1985 would really be like coming out of jail, or whether the prison warders would be with me, the prejudices would remain. In a sentence, I wondered if England would ever be willing and able to pick me against the Australians.

It had been suggested by elements of the media during my suspension that I no longer cared about England. The inferences were that I was indifferent about their results and about my own prospects of playing for them in Test cricket again. This was not only untrue but hurtful and malicious. I never stopped caring about England, never stopped wanting to play at international level, and if my feelings during their winter tour of 1984–85 were confusingly mixed, this was entirely due to my own peculiar predicament.

I always want England to be successful. That is the most important thing to make clear. So, naturally, I was delighted when they achieved what to many people had appeared impossible and retrieved a 1–0 deficit to win a Test series in India, a feat which can only properly be appreciated by those who have taken part in a tour of that demanding country. It was obviously a magnificent team effort and one of which everyone involved, especially captain David Gower, must feel justly proud.

Sitting at home in Essex, with only the radio and the newspapers to help me translate the bare statistics of the matches, I could not accurately assess just how well England played, but what was abundantly plain from figures alone was the considerable part played by the two regular opening batsmen, Tim Robinson and Graeme Fowler.

Before the tour began, it had seemed to many outsiders – myself included – that this was a department in which the team could struggle for consistency. After all, Robinson was a complete newcomer to the Test scene and Fowler, for all his flair and courage against the fast men of the West Indies, could not be considered an established part of the side as his technique outside off-stump was still being persistently questioned. That they were both to emerge with averages of more than 50 from the five Tests, and run aggregates in excess of 400, is testimony to the way they must have worked to adapt to such foreign conditions.

Perhaps the pitches were generally better for batting than had been expected, but let that take nothing away from the men who made the runs. Fowler and Robinson managed to give the innings a thoroughly solid start more often than not, thus allowing Mike Gatting to come in with a platform laid. The difference in his confidence, as he finally justified all his vast but unfulfilled potential with 575 runs in the series, was quite remarkable.

It should not be forgotten that Martyn Moxon of Yorkshire, an opener with impressive technique, played extremely well on the tour whenever he had the chance – but Robinson and Fowler's partnership was so successful that Moxon's opportunities were restricted to four first-class innings, in which he made a total of 231 runs.

Now we come to the crux of my dilemma. Delighted though I was for the side to be winning, it would be dishonest of me to claim glibly that I applauded every run made by the openers. How could I? Each big score they made increased the size of my task in trying to regain my place. I am a patriot, no matter what people may have said about me, and I want England to win every game they play, whether I am involved or not. But perhaps I can be forgiven for the haunting wish that the bulk of the runs had occasionally been made by those a little further down the batting order?

Every time this matter was discussed in the press, I winced when I read references to 'Gooch being an automatic selection' for the 1985 summer or to 'Robinson, Fowler and Moxon contesting only one place against Australia'. Writing just as the season is about to get under way, I do not see things this way at all. I am taking absolutely nothing for granted, because I have no right to return after a three-year enforced break and assume that those who have held the fort will automatically stand aside to let me take up my old position. That would be an unreasonably vain assumption and even if many others appear to be making it, I have no intention of thinking that way.

The way I see it is this. At the start of the 1985 season, the England selectors will have their eyes trained on the scores coming in from around the country. In one sense they will be in a far healthier position than they have been for some years, with an enviable level of competition for almost every place in the team. What it does mean, however, is that they are going to have to start disappointing players again by omitting some who might consider they have perfectly adequate grounds for selection.

Nowhere is the competition fiercer than at the head of the order. I have already mentioned the tourists, Robinson, Fowler and Moxon, none of whom lessened their cause during the winter. Then there are the three who did not make the tour for various reasons – Andy Lloyd, sidelined after being hit on the head by Malcolm Marshall on his Test debut, Paul Terry, recovering from a broken arm, and Chris Broad, who had been controversially left out when the 16 names were drawn up. All three undertook a tour of Zimbabwe with an English Counties team in February, and there can be no doubt that they, too, will be pressing their claims on the selectors come May. Add to this six the openers released from the ban – Wayne Larkins, Dennis Amiss and Geoff Boycott apart from myself – and it can be seen just what a difficult task will confront the selectors in reducing this cast-list to two starters for the opening Test in the Ashes series at Headingley.

The first month of the season is bound to be decisive. Different selectors may have their personal leanings but, so far as I am concerned, everyone will be setting off with an equal chance. I will simply be setting out with the aim of making more runs than any of my competitors so that the selectors cannot ignore me; if I fail during May, then I cannot expect to be chosen. I am very well aware that I have to fight for my England future, and this is the greatest motivation I could possibly have.

I have mentioned earlier that my game occasionally suffered during the three years in the wilderness for a shortage of incentives. Playing for Essex is something I love doing, and always will, but any sportsman worth the description relishes new challenges and wider horizons. These have been taken away from me, but now that they are back I do not intend to allow them to slip from view again.

It is naturally a lingering fear that the past will still be held against me, but I have to try to put that thought out of my mind. I give the selectors credit for wanting to choose the best available players and I believe that if I make the runs to justify it, they will include me in their plans, ignoring what has gone before. Others among the 15 banned players will be starting 1985 with similar ambitions; I know, for instance, just how much my good friend John Emburey now wants to be considered for England again and how he, too, must have suffered from mixed feelings as he heard details of the success enjoyed by his spinning colleagues and competitors Phil Edmonds and Pat Pocock in India. John had spent the winter in Melbourne, playing club cricket and coaching in the schools. Like me, he had found his appetite for touring with England refreshed and recharged by the years of absence and I very much hope that we might link up again in the West Indies during the early months of 1986, five years on from our last trip there, the trip on which we were first sounded out about going to South Africa.

English cricket showed the first hint of a renaissance when David Gower's men won in India, and I tended to take far more notice of that fine result than of the subsequent disappointments in lucrative but relatively ambiguous one-day competitions in Australia and in Sharjah. Despite the efforts of the marketing men, especially in Australia, who try to hype limited-overs matches to the detriment of the five-day game, it is still Test cricket on which any nation is judged – and I hope that will always continue to be the case. There is a certain instant glamour and an undeniable excitement about playing a one-day game in front of a big, noisy crowd; but there is nothing to compare with the prolonged tension of a Test match, nothing that can beat the satisfaction of a hundred in an important five-day contest. I hope to enjoy that feeling again before too long.

Whatever happens to my form when the season begins, no-one can say I have neglected my fitness. By training with West Ham's footballers four mornings a week, pushing myself physically to a degree that most of the cricketers of bygone days would have considered inconceivable, I feel trimmer and stronger than for many a long day. I only hope that it shows in my game.

There is much to look forward to at Essex, where our captain Keith Fletcher, having decided to continue for at least one more year, has deservedly been the recipient of an OBE in the New Year's Honours List. 'Fletch' will have a very familiar squad of players under him, but hopefully improved by the arrival of left-arm spinner John Childs from Gloucestershire and the further development of young talents such as Gladwin, Prichard and Foster.

It promises to be an exciting summer, 1985. Perhaps the most important summer of my career. I plan to go on a good few years yet, you see – but I would like to think that at least some of those years will be spent doing what I like best . . . batting for England.

Statistical appendix

SAB ENGLISH XI AVERAGES – FIRST-CLASS MATCHES

Figures reproduced courtesy of Wisden Cricketers' Almanack 1983 *(Queen Anne Press).*

BATTING

	M	I	NO	R	HS	Avge
D. L. Amiss	4	7	2	308	73*	61.60
G. A. Gooch	4	7	0	396	109	56.57
W. Larkins	4	7	0	231	95	33.00
G. Boycott	4	7	0	204	95	29.14
R. A. Woolmer	4	7	1	168	100	28.00
J. K. Lever	4	5	3	41	10*	20.50
P. Willey	3	4	0	79	39	19.75
A. P. E. Knott	4	6	0	63	27	10.50
C. M. Old	4	6	1	48	20	9.60
L. B. Taylor	3	3	1	10	10*	5.00
D. L. Underwood	2	3	0	14	8	4.66
M. Hendrick	2	2	1	1	1	1.00

Played in one match: J. E. Emburey 13; G. W. Humpage 1, 10. A. Sidebottom did not play in a first-class match.

**Signifies not out.*

BOWLING

	O	M	R	W	Avge
L. B. Taylor	91.3	22	206	11	18.72
J. E. Emburey	47.5	10	153	6	25.50
G. A. Gooch	33	6	114	4	28.50
J. K. Lever	107	25	335	11	30.45
M. Hendrick	61.4	16	144	4	36.00
C. M. Old	102	34	258	5	51.60

Also bowled: G. W. Humpage 2–0–6–0; A. P. E. Knott 1–0–5–0; W. Larkins 11.1–0–47–1; D. L. Underwood 45–10–128–2; P. Willey 4–1–8–0.

FIELDING

A. P. E. Knott 17; G. A. Gooch 6, D. L. Amiss 1, G. Boycott 1, J. E. Emburey 1, M. Hendrick 1, G. W. Humpage 1, C. M. Old 1, P. Willey 1, R. A. Woolmer 1.

GRAHAM GOOCH IN FIRST-CLASS CRICKET

CAREER FIGURES

	M	I	NO	R	HS	Avge	100	50	Ct	R	W	Avge	5	B/B
1973	1	1	0	18	18	18.00	–	–	1	–	–	–		–
1974	15	25	3	637	114*	28.95	1	2	4	153	3	51.00		1/17
1975	24	42	0	1147	100	27.30	1	7	16	113	2	56.50		2/32
1976	21	34	4	1273	136	42.43	3	6	17	334	10	33.40	1	5/40
1977	23	37	6	837	105*	27.00	1	5	11	345	8	43.12		4/60
1978	21	33	3	1254	129	41.80	2	9	22	90	2	45.00		2/33
1978–79	13	23	1	514	74	23.36	–	3	13	80	1	80.00		1/16
1979	17	25	2	838	109	36.43	1	6	28	201	4	50.25		1/10
1979–80	7	14	3	639	115	58.09	1	6	9	113	3	37.66		2/16
1980	19	35	5	1437	205	47.90	6	2	17	367	15	24.46		3/57
1980–81	7	13	0	777	153	59.76	4	1	4	108	1	108.00		1/14
1981	16	31	0	1345	164	43.38	5	5	11	243	6	40.50		3/47
1981–82	13	21	3	967	127	53.72	2	6	10	150	2	75.00		2/12
1981–82	4	7	0	396	109	56.57	1	3	6	114	4	28.50		2/45
1982	23	38	1	1632	149	44.10	3	12	25	541	22	24.59	1	7/14
1982–83	9	18	3	597	126	39.80	2	1	11	86	5	17.20		4/15
1983	26	38	1	1481	174	40.02	4	7	35	572	11	52.00		3/40
1983–84	7	13	1	615	171	51.25	2	1	5	89	3	29.66		2/34
1984	26	45	7	2559	227	67.34	8	13	27	850	38	22.36		4/54
Total	292	493	43	18963	227	42.14	47	95	272	4549	140	32.49	2	7/14

TEST FIGURES

Season	Opponents	Venue	R	1st	2nd	Ct	O	M	R	W	O	M	R	W
1975	Australia	1. Birmingham	L	0	0	1								
		2. Lord's	D	6	31	1								
1978	Pakistan	2. Lord's	W	54		1								
		3. Leeds	D	20		1								
	New Zealand	1. Oval	W	0	91*									
		2. Nottingham	W	55		1								
		3. Lord's	W	2	42*		10	0	29	0				
1978–79	Australia	1. Brisbane	W	2	2	1	1	0	1	0				
		2. Perth	W	1	43	3								
		3. Melbourne	L	25	40									
		4. Sydney	W	18	22	2	5	1	14	0				
		5. Adelaide	W	1	18									
		6. Sydney	W	74		3								
1979	India	1. Birmingham	W	83		4					6	3	8	0
		2. Lord's	D	10			10	5	16	1	2	0	8	0
		3. Leeds	D	4		1	3	1	2	0				
		4. Oval	D	79	31	1	2	0	6	0	2	0	9	0
1979–80	Australia	2. Sydney	L	18	4	1	11	4	16	2	8	2	20	0
		3. Melbourne	L	99	51									
	India	Bombay	W	8	49*	1	4	2	3	0				
1980	West Indies	1. Nottingham	L	17	27		7	2	11	1	2	1	2	0
		2. Lord's	D	123	47	2	7	1	26	0				
		3. Manchester	D	2	26	2								
		4. Oval	D	83	0	1	1	0	2	0				
		5. Leeds	D	14	55		8	3	18	2				
	Australia	Lord's	D	8	16		8	3	16	0				
1980–81	West Indies	1. Port-of-Spain	L	41	5		2	0	3	0				
		3. Bridgetown	L	26	116	2	2	0	13	0				
		4. Antigua	D	33	83		2	2	0	0				
		5. Kingston	D	153	3	1	8	3	20	0				
1981	Australia	1. Nottingham	L	10	6									
		2. Lord's	D	44	20		10	4	28	0				
		3. Leeds	W	2	0									
		4. Birmingham	W	21	21									
		5. Manchester	W	10	5	1								
1981–82	India	1. Bombay	L	2	1									
		2. Bangalore	D	58	40	1								
		3. New Delhi	D	71	20*	1	8.1	1	12	2				
		4. Calcutta	D	47	63	2	6	1	10	0	2	0	4	0
		5. Madras	D	127			9	2	27	0	8	2	24	0
		6. Kanpur	D	58										
	Sri Lanka	Colombo	W	22	31	1								

	M	I	NO	R	HS	100	50	Avge	Ct	O	M	R	W	Avge
Totals	42	75	4	2540	153	4	15	35.77	36	154.1	43	348	8	43.50